The Bible is a *Girl's* Best Friend

SALLY MILLER

HARVEST HOUSE PUBLISHERS

EUGENE, OREGON

Cover photo © Nathan Watkins / iStockphoto

Cover by Garborg Design Works, Savage, Minnesota

THE BIBLE IS A GIRL'S BEST FRIEND
Copyright © 2007 by Sally Miller
Published by Harvest House Publishers
Eugene, Oregon 97402
www.harvesthousepublishers.com

Library of Congress Cataloging-in-Publication Data
   Miller, Sally, 1968-
   The Bible is a girl's best friend / Sally Miller.
      p. cm.
   ISBN-13: 978-0-7369-2029-2 (pbk.)
   ISBN-10: 0-7369-2029-3
   1. Christian women—Religious life. 2. Bible—Criticism, interpretation, etc. I. Title.
   BV4527.M55 2007
   248.8'43—dc22
                                2007002492

Printed in the United States of America

   07 08 09 10 11 12 13 14 15 / VP-SK / 12 11 10 9 8 7 6 5 4 3 2 1

For Mom—
who gave flesh to
Habakkuk and made me love *the Woman at the Well*

Acknowledgments

Bry—whose adventurous spirit brought us to China and back. Thanks for putting up with typing at 5:00 AM and other crazy hours. I'm glad we didn't listen…look how much we would be missin'.

Ben, Ayden, and Emily—my trinity of children—thanks for playing nicely together…most of the time…while Mama wrote.

Mom and Dad—for hanging in there, breaking the chain, and loving your grandkids with a crazed, playful, tireless, gorgeous kind of love.

Billie—for the garden walks! I can't wait for another spring with you.

Rob & Kristin—you are brilliant, encouraging, missional, and hilarious. I'm so blessed to call you family and friends. We can't wait for you to move to Chicago!

My Tribe of Five: Cheri, I couldn't live without your insights, friendship, and long-distance phone calls. You are priceless, treasured, and irreplaceable. Margie, you are a wise and wondrous woman who regularly brings me closer to Jesus. Heather, thanks for making me laugh and for praying for me. Oh, how I will miss your mom! Beth, it has been a joy to watch your new life and marriage blossom. Blessed be the Lord! Julie, my sister in adoption, welcome to motherhood. I can't wait to share the journey with you.

Unexpected friends who have shown up in the corners of my life and on my doorstep—Laura, Lisa, Sandy, Renee, Sara, Beth, Suzie, Michelle, Lynn, Julie, Robin, Terry, and Judy. You are all dear and valuable to me in daily, organic, sustaining ways. Thanks a million!

Terry Glaspey and Barb Sherrill—thanks for Spumoni and Spavone's, and for entering into the wildness of postmodern faith with me. Once again I appreciate your gracious, informed guidance, Terry.

Carolyn McCready, who looks pretty in pink and should be careful about her offers to provide a writing refuge in Oregon. I appreciate your Spirit of Nurture and Shoring Up.

Barb Gordon, my adept, thorough, communicative editor who swims with dolphins and speaks Spanish. You're the best! Vaya con Dios.

My phenomenal Harvest House family. I literally couldn't do it without you. God bless!

To the ministers and friends at Blanchard Road: Sue Roman, Amanda Jethani, Marcella Lewis, Mary Huizinga, Dale and Kim Showalter, Brad and Dawn Jones, Kristen Mapstone, Pastor John Casey, Pastor Skye Jethani, Mary Ellen Slefinger, Tim and Kelly Johnson, Ken and Tina Kunz. You have been Christ to my family and me. For this I am grateful.

Contents

Why Did the Bible Seem Like a Relic? 9

1. Getting to Know You 13
   Meeting God in His Word

2. Word Balloons 21
   The Bible—Living, Breathing, Buoyant

3. Touch, Smell, Taste, Read, and See 29
   God's Word as Tangible Love

4. Heart Scribbles 37
   The Bible as a Love Letter

5. You Can Call Me… 45
   The Bible Giving Names

6. A Theme Runs Through It 53
   God's Word Brings Meaning to Our Lives

7. Great Physicians 61
   God's Word Heals

8. Frequent Flyers 69
   The Bible Takes Us on a Journey

9. Family Ties 77
   God's Word Offers Inclusion

10. Red Reminders 83
    Life-Changing Symbols

11. Loving Your Neighbor 89
    The Bible Moving in Next Door

12. A True Page-Turner 95
    Wisdom, Mercy, and Incredible Stories

13. I Give You My Word 101
    God's Word Holds Promises

14. Glow Sticks 107
    The Bible as Illuminator

15. Spices, Perfumes, Stories 115
    The Bible Caring for Our Needs

16. Filling in the Blanks 123
    Scripture Knows Our Stories

17. Unexpected Friends 131
    The Bible, a Book of Surprises

18. Expectant Friends 137
    Waiting with the Word

19. Freedom Within Boundaries 143
    The Bible as Creative Parent

20. Soul Spa 149
    God's Rejuvenating Word

21. Dream Catchers 159
    Absorbing Truth Even as We Sleep

22. God's Garden 167
    The Bible as Botanical

23. Sustaining Meals 173
    The Bible as Daily Bread

24. Home 179
    The Bible Dwelling in Us

25. Eyes 185
    The Bible as a Way to See Christ

26. Rock Writing 191
    The Bible Gives Good, Solid Words

27. Open Arms 197
    Embracing and Embraced by the Word

28. Shared Stories 203
    God's Word Connects Us

    Epilogue 211

    Notes 213

Why Did the Bible Seem Like a Relic?

Readin' Mom's Biblical Bridal Bouquet

Bibles have always fascinated, intrigued, even mesmerized me. My family knows this. So when grandmas, grandpas, great uncles, and aunts pass away, I'm inevitably the one who gets their often dusty Holy Bibles. The tomes tower in a stack beside my writing desk, including Aunt Muriel's—exploding with cards, notes, dried flowers, etc. and Grandma Norberg's thick, burgundy Life Application Study Bible, to name just two.

Even as a little girl I was obsessed with Bibles. I remember sitting pretzel style in our sunny family room, paging through my father's illuminated Catholic version. I sniffed its gilded parchment pages and studied its maps and concordance for hours. My favorite Bible, though, was Mom's tiny, tattered Authorized King James. She carried it on her wedding day—a biblical bridal bouquet. Inside its front cover is the following inscription.

To Carol

From your godmother, Aunt Phil

When I was four years old, in shaky, unsure, elementary school handwriting, I added five letters to that inscription: S-A-L-L-Y. The addition was proof that I too wanted ownership of this book that held secrets and stories, marvels and mysteries, power and paradox.

I remember trying to read the King James' microscopic words—especially the ones Mom had underlined in red, blue, or black pen. I turned pages thinner than the wings of a butterfly over and over trying to decode her annotations. Repeatedly I read her dog-eared pages hoping to squeeze out some wonder and wisdom. But inspiration and knowledge eluded me no matter how many times I read.

Pluggin' and Chuggin' with Inductive Study

Years later, when I was in junior high, my longing to understand the Bible was still not slaked. Pam, a teacher, friend, and mentor, invited me to a before-school Bible study. She taught me about *inductive study:* answering a series of questions about given chapters and verses, paraphrasing passages, and applying them practically.

There's no doubt that this method, along with my favorite Ryrie Study Bible, a concordance, and Bible dictionary, unlocked secrets to God's Word that I never imagined. I learned the Gospels are four re-tellings of Jesus' life, and that the writers are often metaphorically compared to the seasons. I discovered that the psalms are really *songs* meant to be sung. And the epistles (Galatians, Ephesians, Colossians, 1 and 2 Corinthians, to name a few) were written as *letters* of encouragement for the early church.

My bookcases now hold dozens of journals containing notes from years of inductive study. (In fact, I use inductive methods even today.) Still, there was a huge piece missing in my reading of God's messages. Deep within my soul I knew something magical, magnificent, and meaningful would someday unlock the mysteries bound in the leather bindings. Inductive study whet my appetite for the adventure waiting on parchment pages. It nudged me to consider the Bible as more than just an antiquated text. But it was something strange and unexpected that showed me how vibrant, liberating, and expansive the Bible really is.

What My Girlfriends Taught Me

After writing *Girl Talk...God Talk,* a book that chronicles ways our friends can teach us to pray, I gradually realized that for years my relationships with girlfriends have also helped refresh the way I read the Bible. Through their insights and sharing, I now realize that The Book is deeply penetrating, real, fluid, organic, and pertinent. They've helped me see how God's words are alive, fresh, funny, freeing. Because of zany, caring friends who have challenged and walked through life with me since college, I know the Bible is not a book that narrows, limits, prohibits. It enlarges! Catches us off guard. Hits the spot. Knows us better than we know ourselves—just like a good friend!

Our Bibles travel with us through life just like our girlfriends do. So instead of forcing God's Word into an Anglo-Saxon, church-bound box, I want to free the Bible to be part of my daily life. I desire to read it fresh, in the same way I listen to a sonata, watch a sunset, or linger over brew with a friend. I want to return to it again and again during times of sadness, joy, exhaustion, and pain. Sometimes it whispers truths to me. Other times it shouts with joy.

One of the biggest mistakes people make, I think, is to interpret the Word of God strictly, dryly, and dogmatically, as if it were a handbook of do's and don'ts. That's not what the Bible is. Though it *does* contain the Ten Commandments, Levitical law, and practical instructions for Christian living, the Bible is about so much more than rules and regulations. It's a literary, historic, poetic master-piece filled with the drama of pursuing love, good conquering evil, and grace reigning. It's filled with stories of family and friends—true community with all the mess and mire of humanity. And it's ultimately about wondrous words of love and promise found in daily connection with God, the Creator of every story, word, event, and person.

It's so freeing to let go of the Bible as an instruction manual and to experience it as a faithful, drama-filled friend. With our girlfriends we take brisk walks, eat pints of Ben & Jerry's ice cream, light candles, and linger over Starbucks' brew. In each other's lives we serve a variety of roles: comforter, truth-teller, inspirer, teacher, healer, promise holder, storyteller, challenger, hope-giver.

Surprisingly enough, the Bible serves similar roles in our lives. Maybe this sounds strange or irreverent to you. It may even feel a little weird comparing the Bible's roles in our lives to the roles of our girlfriends. I'm not minimizing the holy, perfect, mighty words of God. Instead I want to unveil the *living* and *active ways* God speaks to us through Scripture. The intent is to free us to take our Bibles beyond doctrine-stymied studies and into parks, coffee shops, front porches, and overstuffed fireside chairs. Then maybe we'll discover that God's Word speaks to us like the flowers, frogs, sunsets, and even our best friends do.

The Bible Is a Girl's Best Friend explores myriad stories about friends that shed light on our lives and, ultimately, on the Bible. Each chapter includes three sections:

> *Her Word:* A story about friendship
>
> *God's Word:* How we see the Bible based on the story
>
> *Our Word:* Scriptures, Insights, & Suggestions

Seeing Scripture through the lens of friendship opens our hearts to read between the lines. It lets us see the way a book written more than 2,000 years ago is still relevant today. It broadens our experience of reading the Bible to a wondrous, imaginative, practical, penetrating fullness. And it opens us to deeply see, hear, read, and know God.

> *The word of God is living and active.*
>
> HEBREWS 4:12

Getting to Know You

Meeting God in His Word

I love introducing my friends to each other.
As friends meet friends and become friends the circles
form a beautifully linked chain. The friendship that
Luci and I have has enriched both of us because
of our sharing of friends, because of the marvelous
principle of the "transfer of affection."[1]

MADELEINE L'ENGLE

Her Word—*Meeting Beth*

When I sent my son, Ben, out into the world—to Washington Elementary School—I never imagined all the ways he'd learn and grow and change. Since kindergarten started, he's become an Integer Adder, a Pattern Detective, and, most importantly, a friend. Each and every school day when I meet Ben at the bus stop, he traipses down the stairs of the big yellow bus carrying a backpack and tales of Matthew, "The Boy Who Loves *Star Wars*."

My heart melts as I imagine the mysterious transmutation that has turned mere boys into friends. I can almost see the Divine Alchemist at work during science, recess, and story time, taking ordinary moments and making them extraordinary, turning base metals into gold.

Surprisingly enough, the Divine Alchemist recently rendered gold in my life too. Through Ben and Matthew, I started a friendship with Beth, mom of "*Star Wars* lover." I never dreamed my circle of friendship would enlarge via my son, but it has!

Last fall when Beth came to pick Matthew up from a play-date, she and I started gabbing and gabbing and gabbing and gabbing. The boys stood impatiently by our sides at the front door, hoping the hen party would end. It didn't. Our cock-a-doodle-dooing continued until my husband came home. Before Bryan knew it, Beth and I handed the care-for-the-kids baton to him, slapped on some sneakers, and headed out for a walk. During our aerobic communion, we shared stories traversing our careers as teachers, our families of origin, our sex lives, our church lives. When we returned, sweaty and sore-footed, Ben and Matthew had had enough of each other. But we hadn't.

So with some cajoling, we convinced the boys how fun it'd be if Matthew and his mom stayed for dinner. Over pasta, Beth and I realized we'd be sharing the role of "Art Smart Lady" for the boys' class (bringing prints by Van Gogh, Toulouse-Lautrec, Monet, Manet, and others to be seen, explored, interacted with, experienced). We also realized our husbands have a lot in common: both are lovers of eclectic music and woodworking.

Since then, Beth and I have traded sniffles for coughs when negotiating play-dates. We've swapped stories over lunch at the local McDonald's while our kids played in the Play Land. I even reluctantly donned a swimsuit in order to experience a joint family vacation at a Wisconsin Dell's water park. (Anyone who can get me into swimwear must be a good friend.) Our familial gangs have also broken bread in each other's homes.

Dinner at Beth's is like being invited into the pages of *Better Homes and Gardens*. The first time I was welcomed into her abode I realized that in addition to being lighthearted, bright, hilarious, and honest, Beth also has an artful and keen eye for décor. She knows how to arrange furniture and use color, texture, lighting, and fabric to create friendly, appealing spaces. The wedding of Beth's gifts of design to her husband's woodworking skills is beautiful and utilitarian. Almost every room in my friend's house has an armoire, crib, table, or cabinet that Jeff crafted. The pieces exist in perfect amity with pillows, curtains, and throws (sewn by Beth of course).

One evening this winter my family sat at Jeff, Beth, and Matthew's rustic pine table sharing a burn-the-roof-of-your-mouth hot, oozy, Chicago-style pizza. Jeff told stories of three buddies he's known forever. We followed his tales like stormchasers seeking lightning bolts or bellowing twisters. The wild wind of stories about road trips and campouts enraptured us.

When I asked Jeff where he and his buds met, his answer was matter-of-fact: "In kindergarten at Washington School." In an instant thousands of tiny, shivering bumps covered my arms and legs. I prayed that God would bless Ben and Matthew with crazy, campy, muddy, ruddy, lifelong friendships like Jeff had. I also prayed that Beth and I would have a friendship forged of the same organic stuff.

Just a few weeks ago, I made a loaf of Amish Friendship Bread for Beth. On her doorstep I placed the loaf and some of its starter. Along with the yeasty offering, I left this note and poem:

Dear Beth,

This poem and Friendship Bread are my ways of expressing the bursting, growing, fragrant joys of getting to know you and your son, and then your husband, through my son this year! Thanks for bringing lightness and life to my days as a Washington Elementary School mom!

Leavening

Like yeast in a dark warm place
They grew beneath our hearts
By milk and sweet love

They rose and plumped:
Little Loaves

They enlarged, enlarging us

Into the world they sojourned
On hill, in hall, or home
Sparked by Light
Surrounded in New Story:
Bread Breaking

Boys communing, we commune

Just like Jesus and His friends
On the mountaintop
Where He multiplied
Fish and Loaves

Leavening us

God's Word—*Leavening for Life*

> *I was lying on my couch one night, reading a book about friendship by Beth Kephart...There I lay, listing all [my] friendships...and I felt gratitude...Felt the weight of it like a fog settling in over my stomach, felt it filling me, heavy the way fruit fills a basket. Lying on my couch, I could not believe God had given me all these people to love...I slept on the couch then, blanketed by the weight of my gratitude, Beth Kephart's book under my pillow.[2]*
>
> LAUREN WINNER

At the end of many difficult days, I've fallen asleep with the Bible under my pillow grateful for its palpable presence, its comforting company, and its osmotic message. It often surprises me how unpredictable passages find their way into my heart just like my unexpected acquaintance with Beth has. I'm grateful to be getting to know both Beth and the Bible.

As a Christian public speaker, I love having opportunities to hear women's stories of fresh, virgin encounters with God's Word. Some say they first cracked the Bible during a sad, lonely time in a hotel (thanks to the Gideons). Others mention they received their first Bibles as gifts from friends or as heirlooms from deceased relatives. Most of them agree that getting to know the Bible is a lot like getting to know a new friend.

At first we learn about our friend's favorite color, the way she likes her coffee, her favorite pet peeves. With the Bible, we note the division of Old and New Testaments. We also may explore the genres of biblical books: proverbs (wise sayings), epistles (letters), psalms (songs), gospels (stories about the life of Jesus). Then we learn about authorship, historical context, and themes. As seasons and years go by, we're able to experience deeper layers of knowing. We're able to see facets of God's Word in much the same way we experience shades and dimensions of our friends' personalities.

When I began my journey of getting to know God's Word, one woman was particularly helpful. She was my junior high music teacher, mentor, and friend. Pam noticed my hunger to read and understand the Bible and invited me to a before-school Bible study. With the muscle-twitching anticipation of a racer at the starting block, I accepted her offer. During our early morning moments, Pam schooled my spirit. With practical, tried-and-true methods, she took words that seemed distant and elusive to me and brought them near enough to touch.

First Pam told me to get a good study Bible. I chose a Ryrie. (More than 25 years later, it is still one of my favorite study tools. Though it's now covered in clear packing tape to hold the spine together, I still turn to that "dinosaur" time and again.) Pam also told me to invest in a Bible dictionary. I found the Holman to be particularly useful, especially when I wanted to look up words such as Hellenism, Gnosticism, frontlets, Gilead, grace, redemption, salvation, sanctification, and Zion.

I feel slightly embarrassed to admit that in my overzealousness to read through the Bible in those days I began in Genesis. During several discouraging months, I read page after "dry" page on my way toward the even drier Levitical law. Thankfully Pam let me know that it was O.K. to skip around on my journey through the Bible. She recommended that I begin with the Gospel of John. She told me that if I read Jesus' story, as told by his best bud, all of the Bible would make more sense and mean more to me. She was right. I read John at least five times before venturing again into the deeper waters of the Old Testament.

Pam also recommended that I find a "Through the Bible in a Year calendar." To be honest, I've never actually made it through the entire Bible in one year. I have learned that the calendar is my helper not my master. Happily, for the last *three* years, I've been sallying my way through Robert Murray McCheyne's *Daily Bible Calendar*. When I'm not excited about a word study, intoxicated by a devotional, or following the tangent projected by some Scripture memory or other biblical pursuit, I use the calendar to guide my reading. Consistent study has a way of providing breadth, variety, and depth to my understanding.

Pam taught me a few other illuminating practices worth sharing. One was to ask God to open my eyes each time I begin to read His Word. Because of her suggestion, I memorized Psalm 119:18: "Open my eyes that I may see wonderful things in your law." Each time I crack open my Bible, I pray that sweet, enlarging verse. As I do, I expect God to help me find wonders I'm unable to discover on my own. Pam also recommended that I read large chunks of Scripture, and that I memorize a few favorite verses. (Currently I'm working my way—at a snail's pace—through Romans 8.) When I do this I feel as if the words are with me and in me, becoming part of my life.

Instead of reading the Bible the "right and proper" way and

fearing I'd rip a page or get errant pen markings in the margins, I began to unabashedly love and enjoy God's Word. I started taking my Bible to church, on vacations, to my summer job at Lake Bluff Beach, to school in my backpack, and even to bed with me. I read almost every day—not out of obligation, but out of wildfire desire. I underlined themes, circled recurring words, and wrote related poetry, ideas, references, thoughts, and prayers in the margins. I went crazy with colored pencils and highlighters on the parchment pages.

As I share what I've learned with you and we explore God's Word, I hope you'll realize more and more that our relationship with God's Word develops in much the same way our relationships with girlfriends grow. Whether we've opened The Book one time or one thousand times, the journey can be joyful, intriguing, organic. We don't need to worry if, during certain seasons, Scripture feels like a sticky, wet, amorphous blob of dough in our hands. When it does, we can apply one or more of Pam's ideas. Or we can simply ask God to add some leavening. With divine, flour-laced hands, He'll proof, knead, and fire the dough until it becomes a fragrant and sustaining loaf. And in surprising, supernatural ways we'll find ourselves leavened too.

A little leaven leavens the whole lump of dough.

GALATIANS 5:9 NASB

Our Word—*Scriptures, Insights, & Suggestions*

[Woman] does not live on bread alone, but on every word that comes from the mouth of God.

MATTHEW 4:4

1. If you're hungry for some new, leavening ways of experiencing God's Word, try these: Read a chunk of the Bible and jot down some of your observations and epiphanies in a journal. Read with a friend—ask God to open your eyes to "behold wondrous things in [His] law." Read a shorter book of the Bible such as 1 John, James, Jonah, and Esther every day for a week.

2. The next time you're online, search for some complimentary "Through the Bible in a Year" calendars. Here are three I found: www.backtothebible.org/devotions/journey, www.bible readthrough.com, and www.hebronlutheran.org/Year/ReadThe Bibleinayear.htm.

3. If you're desiring fresh insights in your Bible reading, go to the library or your local Christian bookstore and check out some Bible dictionaries, study Bibles, and other biblical resources.

> *I know that one of the great needs among Christians today is simply the reading of large portions of Scripture…Read it without trying to fit it into established categories. Expect to hear new things in new ways. Keep a journal of your findings.*[3]
>
> RICHARD J. FOSTER

Word Balloons

The Bible—Living,
Breathing, Buoyant

> *Words written fifty years ago, a hundred years ago,*
> *a thousand years ago, can have as much of this power*
> *today as ever they had it then, to come alive for us and in*
> *us and to make us more alive within ourselves.*
> *That, I suppose, is the final mystery as well as the final*
> *power of words: that not even across great*
> *distances of time and space do they ever lose their capacity*
> *for becoming incarnate.*[1]

FREDERICK BUECHNER

Her Word—*Cheri, A Woman of Words*

My writer friend Cheri loves language. She gathers words in her mind the way my sons collect rocks. She believes words have an energy and breath that moves, motivates, makes real. Recently Cheri was asked to speak about her career as a writer by her daughter Jen's teacher. With mutual giddiness, Cheri and I ruminated—via phone—over stories, writing exercises, and poems that might acknowledge and ignite the love of words in Jen and her third-grade classmates.

Cheri began the conversation with me, joy bubbling up in her voice: "I want to do something with the five senses, maybe something…"

Motivated by my own passion for words, I interrupted, "You could do an entire lesson on simile, Cher. You could quote the Jack Prelutsky poem *A Pizza the Size of the Sun*. Or you could explore opposites. Maybe you'd want to use this corny poem I wrote the other day. Do ya want to hear it?"

"Sure."

After shuffling through a pile of scrap paper, I found the poem on the back of a Rosati's Pizza menu. "Here goes:

> *white, black, young, old*
> *noisy, silent, warm, cold*
> *tall, short, high, low*
> *silken, bumpy, fast, slow*
>
> *soft, hard, wrong, right*
> *wakeful, sleepy, day, night*
> *thick, thin, smile, frown*
> *over, under, up, down*
>
> *rough, smooth, in, out,*
> *liquid, solid, sing, shout…*

"All right already, Sal. I think I get the idea," Cher interrupted. "That doesn't really resonate with me. I was imagining something a little more simplistic…less didactic."

I tried to shift gears but found myself grinding because of the long-lived teacher in me. "You could introduce Haiku, onomatopoeia, free-verse, metaphor, meter, form. It could be a workshop on…"

"Sal…Sal…Sal," Cher said, quashing my textbook ramblings. "Remember, Jen and her classmates are *third graders*."

"Oh, yeah. Third graders," I mumbled.

"I love your ideas, Sal. But I think I'll just stick with words. Plain old words," Cher stated.

I wondered why I hadn't thought of that perfectly simple, obvious-yet-deep lesson bursting with possibilities. "That's brilliant!" I said.

Just then I heard Cheri's youngest son crying. "Thanks for your help, Sal. Sean's up from his nap...gotta go."

Before the receiver clicked, I squeezed in, "Call me and let me know how it goes!"

After I hung up, I thought about Cheri's idea. I knew she had experienced the profundity and power of words. I also knew her gentle, gracing, honest way with children. I imagined how inspirational her classroom visit would be.

A week later I was folding laundry when my phone rang. It was Cher, ready to relate details about the "word work."

"How'd it go?" I asked as I finished folding a pair of Ben's jeans and turned my attention toward a tangle of towels.

"I entered the room with a multicolored balloon bouquet. On each of the balloons I had written a word: *wiggle, smell, black, monster, sunshine, firefly, laugh, love, deep.* The kids were squealing, wiggling, pointing, trying to read all the balloons, including the ones at the back of the bouquet: *pickle, Scooby Doo, kick, snort, burp.*"

"I love it," I said, visualizing the floating orbs and the buoyancy of the classroom.

"We sat in the story corner," Cher continued. "I asked, 'How do balloons make you feel?' Their answers blew me away: 'happy, floating, excited, like a party or something good is going to happen, creative.' Can you believe it? One of the kids actually said 'creative'!"

I stopped folding towels and sat still as a portrait on my love seat. "Children always have a way of cutting right to the heart of things, don't they?" I responded.

"Absolutely! They have a way of affirming everything I believe.

Following their lead, I told them that words make me feel the same way too. I explained that as a writer, words are my tools. I use them to help other people see life and themselves in fresh, true ways that help them be more aware, awake, alive."

Cheri told me she had the students list their 10 favorite words and then combine them based on their sounds, feelings, and meanings (paying no attention to any rules). She told the kids to try the words on as if they were pieces of clothing. "Just mix and match," she encouraged. With their lists, the children created poems: funny poems, true poems, touching poems. At the end of the class they shared their poetry with one another. I imagined the classroom filled with sparkling-eyed, giggly, wiggly students alive with the wonder of working with words.

God's Word—*The Word Afloat*

> *And when...words tell of virtue and nobility,*
> *when they move us closer to that truth and gentleness of*
> *spirit by which we become fully human, the reading*
> *of them is sacramental; and a library is as holy a place as*
> *any temple is holy because through the words which are*
> *treasured in it the Word itself becomes flesh again and*
> *again and dwells among us and within us,*
> *full of grace and truth.*[2]
>
> FREDERICK BUECHNER

Every time we read the Bible we can experience a holy moment—like the one in Jen's classroom. This does not happen just because the Bible is a sacred text, but because it's also full of words as wild, winsome, wacky, and wise as the ones on Cheri's balloons. Buoyed by the Holy Spirit, Scripture has a life of its own: moving, blowing, swirling about us. When we read the words, we see ourselves and God more clearly. We can be transformed into *real,* alive, free, breathing women. When Paul wrote that the Word of God is *living* and *active,* I think he was picturing something as buoyant and beautiful as Cheri's balloon bouquet (Hebrews 4:12).

Granted, the Bible didn't always seem as light and airy as a balloon to me. I clearly remember studies of prophecy and war concerning the "Divided Kingdom" in Daniel when the Bible felt archaic, dusty, and leaden. It was then that my friend Deb suggested a few ways to make Bible reading more meaningful, touching, and real.

First, Deb said, "Try reading the epistles as if they were love letters written just for you. Read the psalms like a diary. And when you read the parables of Jesus, pretend you're one of the main characters in the stories."

On another occasion, over triple-berry pie at Baker's Square, Deb gave me the best advice ever: "When you read a passage addressed to Israel, substitute your name any time you come across Israel's. For example Psalm 73:1, 'Surely God is good to Israel,' would read, 'Surely God is good to *Sally.*' Or, 'Hear, O Israel: The LORD our God, the LORD is one. Love the LORD your God with all your heart and with all your soul and with all your strength' (Deuteronomy 6:4-5), would read, 'Hear, O *Sally:* The LORD our God, the LORD is one...' "

These methods have helped me experience A.W. Tozer's "happy moment when the Spirit begins to illuminate the Scriptures." These moments occur when inked words on parchment become as "warm and intimate and clear as the word of a dear friend." The words dance and dwell with us. They make us feel as if something good is about to happen, something like a balloon-festooned party.

Recently, after years of using Deb's methods to awaken me to God's words, I was watching *Oprah.* The show was about the "lost baby girls of China." It explained that thousands of infant girls are abandoned in railroad stations, grocery markets, and parks in China each year. This occurs partly because of China's population regulations and partly because of a cultural preference for sons. Orphanages in China are overflowing with female babies.

I was riveted by Oprah's coverage because my husband, Bryan, and I were, at the time, in the process of adopting a little girl from China. After the *Oprah* show, I pictured my little shiny black-lacquered-hair girl needing me for a bottle or diaper change. I imagined snuggling her and feeding her Cream of Wheat. I wept for my daughter, alive in China, waiting for me. I also cried for the others who'd be left behind when my baby came home.

The morning after seeing the *Oprah* show, I felt God nudging me to spend some time reading His Word. I could tell He wanted me to clothe myself in words like Jen and her classmates had. To be honest, I was a little ticked at God, wondering what He planned on doing for all the precious, abandoned babes of the world. So I resisted His invitation. I got out of bed at 5:30 AM, as I usually do. But instead of accepting His welcome to read and be "dressed" in His Word, I put on my robe, made coffee, did two loads of laundry, wrote some notes for one of my books, and lit a fire.

God's still, soft voice kept nudging me: *"Read, Sally. Just pick up My Word, and start reading where you left off last."* Expecting nothing, I finally flopped my Bible open to Ezekiel 16:4-8 and read:

> On the day you were born...you were not washed with water to make you clean, nor were you...wrapped in cloths...Rather, you were thrown out into the open field, for on the day you were born you were despised.
>
> I passed by and saw you kicking about in your blood, and as you lay there...I said to you, "Live!" I made you grow like a plant of the field. You grew up...and became the most beautiful of jewels...and when I looked at you and saw that you were old enough for love, I spread the corner of my garment over you...I gave you my solemn oath and entered into a covenant with you...and you became mine.

Wet, saline lines marked my face as I realized that these verses were God's sentiments toward my daughter. Through this prophecy for Israel, I recognized God's words as powerful, breathing promises to take care of China's lost daughters…and *all* the abandoned babies of the world.

Thanks to Cheri and Deb, I realize that God's words are living and buoyant. They're as vibrant, virile, and viable today as they were in first-century Palestine. They're as radical, real, and relevant now as they were in the days of ancient Egypt. They apply to China, America, Deb, Cheri, Jen's third-grade class, you, me, and everyone else. They give us hope that God will walk into the corners of our lives holding the strings to a rainbow-colored balloon bouquet inscribed with words such as *hope, help, healing, family, friends, inclusion, grace, peace, truth, art, beauty, books,* and *music.* Whatever the words, I know they'll make us feel as if something creative and good is about to happen.

> *God did not write a book and send it by messenger*
> *to be read at a distance by unaided minds.*
> *He spoke a Book and lives in His spoken words,*
> *constantly speaking His words and causing the power of*
> *them to persist across the years.*[3]
>
> A.W. TOZER

Our Word—*Scripture, Insights, & Suggestions*

1. What is your relationship with words? Do you enjoy them like Cheri does? Do they challenge, elude, or frustrate you?

2. What words would be on God's balloon bouquet for you? List them. Then look up their definitions in a dictionary. How do these words breathe life into you?

3. Have you experienced the way God's Word is a living, breathing book? Explain this to a friend or journal about this.

4. Read John, chapter 1. Think about what it means when the Bible says, "The Word became flesh and made his dwelling among us." How many ways did Jesus become the Word? Write a poem, paint a picture, or take a photograph that expresses this incarnational truth for you.

> *The Word became flesh and made his dwelling among us. We have seen his glory, the glory of the One and Only, who came from the Father, full of grace and truth.*
>
> JOHN 1:14

Touch, Smell, Taste, Read, and See

God's Word as Tangible Love

The two times in my life with my husband where his body was most totally an icon for me was on our wedding night, and on the morning of his death...
The human body, that which Jesus honoured in his own flesh, can be a beautiful icon of the love of God, the body in its entirety, the eyes, the toenails, the body hair—every single part.[1]

MADELEINE L'ENGLE

Her Word—*Bryan's Bod*

I love my husband's body. Bryan's six-foot-four-inch frame, thickly calloused hands, floppy golden hair, ice-blue eyes, and the way his butt looks in a pair of blue jeans intoxicate me. A carpenter by trade and frat boy by disposition, he's an unlikely *and* perfect match for me. Before meeting Bry I dated singers, Bible students, church men with visions of building God's kingdom from behind a desk, pulpit, or piano. Bry, on the other hand, smells of freshly cut wood because he builds stairs, mantels, crown moldings, and homes. Though he once made a beautiful dovetailed box for me,

Bry helps me live outside the box in a place of limitless, tangible love.

My hubby and I first met—victims of his sister's neighbor's Cupid arrow—via the phone. For several weeks we talked hour on end about everything from collegiate days to worldviews to relationships with families of origin. (He comes from a tribe of seven, so we had plenty about which to talk!) He always made me laugh and think. I looked forward to more phone conversations. When we finally met face-to-face, I was struck by his height, flannel shirt, ripped jeans, and masculinity.

In a crowded restaurant's vestibule we had our first hug. Overwhelmed by his sinewy arms, shoulders, and back, I almost fell to the floor. In a daze I imagined friends resuscitating my breathless body, pulling me to my feet only to reveal my pomegranate-red face. A strong, independent woman, I was confused and flustered by the way I felt in Bry's presence. He had a way of waking up my senses and bringing out the excited little girl in me. At the same time, he gently and consistently pursued me, helping me feel safe in the circle of his affection.

When we were dating, I was actually scared of Bry's steadfast commitment to me. I remember being afraid of *falling* in love with him because it felt as if I were literally falling, being pulled by gravity to an ultimate earthly and embarrassing thud. At the same time, I couldn't wait to hold his rough hands, look into his eyes (so different in color from my chocolate browns), and smell his salty Aramis cologne. Something about being near Bryan calmed, comforted, and warmed me like a hand-knit scarf on a chilly day.

It's funny, but after being together for more than a decade, I still get excited when I see Bryan's truck on the road or his cell number pop up on our caller ID. For years I waited for Bryan. I hated being single: eating meals alone, sleeping solo, making coffee in a one-cup pot. I longed to connect with someone different yet complementary to me, someone who could show me the masculine side of God. Bryan does that. He's a partner, friend, lover, spouse who brings me steaming mugs of coffee (from a huge pot) in the morning, calms my often-hostile argumentative personality with a touch of his hand, saves me (and my degenerating back) from unloading groceries, carries boxes of books, and edges our gardens. He's an icon of God's strong, steadfast, protective, pursuing love.

Even though neither of us currently fits into our nuptial attire, surprisingly we still fit together perfectly. My head rests on the pad of his pectoral muscles when I need a nuzzle or the cotton of his T-shirt to wipe away tears. His arm drapes around my shoulders during a movie. Our ideas about marriage, spirituality, and parenting dovetail like the corners of his well-made boxes. Our bodies rest like ladles nesting—at least when our mattress isn't also laden with three little teaspoons.

Maybe it sounds irreverent, but my husband's body (every inch of it) is a perfect representation of God's love for me. Sensually experiencing the pleasure of his warm baritone whispers, the laughter and lovin' of our marriage bed, the tickle of his auburn whiskers during our end-of-the-day kisses remind me of the ever-present, penetrating, pleasing ways God is my Husband. Even the prophet Isaiah acknowledges God's marital role in the life of a Christian: "For your Maker is your husband—the LORD Almighty is his name" (Isaiah 54:5).

Recently Bryan and I had an experience with physical loving that, though not sexually charged, nearly rivaled the intensity and wonder of our wedding night. After months of carrying postage-stamp-sized pictures of an apple-cheeked baby girl from China, we traveled to JiangXi province to meet our daughter for the first time. Our arms ached to hold her chubby body. Our lips longed to kiss her soft, brown-berry skin. Standing on foreign soil in a Social Welfare Institute we were anxious aliens until, at last, we were united face-to-face, skin-to-skin, with a crying, almond-eyed baby with curly eyelashes.

In much the same way as Bry and I connect through a physical, daily relationship, we now connect with our baby, Emily, touching her black, shiny hair...tasting salt while kissing her tear-streaked cheeks...beholding her first, tentative, sweet smiles...holding her with arms that promise to never let go. In a holy moment with Bry and Emily, it has become ineffably clear to me that God has given us the ability to love with hearts and hands. That's why He dreamed up friendship and marriage and family: places where we can love one another and experience His love, in tangible, touching ways.

> *An icon, for me, is an open window to God.*
> *An icon is something I can look through and get a*
> *wider glimpse of God.*[2]
>
> MADELEINE L'ENGLE

God's Word—*Touching and Being Touched*

> *The Bible is the love story of God with His people.*
> *God calls, pursues, forgives and heals.*
> *Our response to His love is itself His gift.*[3]
>
> BRENNAN MANNING

Just as Bryan's body is an icon of God's love for me, so is the Bible. God knows we live in a world made of physical matter: atoms, neutrons, electrons, particles. He also knows that because of our material existence we need tangible, sensory proof of His love and presence in our lives. That's one of the reasons He offers husbands, family, friends, bread, wine, crosses, art, music, sunsets, sundaes, swimming holes, and the Bible. Freely and daily God gives us tasteable, seeable, touchable, hearable, smellable representations of His love.

The Bible is one of these symbols—or icons—that remind us of God's promises to be faithful to us and to love us. Words on paper. Stories in cotton or leather bindings. We can read His words, hold His Book in our hands, even go to sleep with it beneath our pillows. I get excited just touching and flipping through the Bible's parchment pages. It's as if they're whispering secret messages to me.

As a writer, I have a strong attraction to anything made of paper. I like the feel of it and the look of it. As a child, I remember even liking the taste of it (ripped and savored in tiny pieces, of course). And, ahhhhhh, the smell of it! Have you ever caught a whiff of brand-new books hot off the printing press? What could be better? I think a new, leather-bound Bible has an equally intoxicating scent. I'd *almost* rather smell that than a pie in the oven, freshly cut grass, or Shalimar.

I confess I have a difficult time throwing away paper products. I keep receipts, stage bills, maps, bookmarks, MapQuest printouts, photos (even bad ones), notes scribbled on scratch paper, birthday cards, grocery lists, wrapping paper, tissue paper, specialty paper, copy paper, and newspaper. I regularly beg Cheri to come to my writing room and help me dispose of paper. She refuses, telling me that if I'd stop linking memories to stupid snippets, I might be able to let go of my white-knuckled grip on scraps.

Admittedly, she's right. Each tattered piece of paper represents a moment in time, a sweet memory. Sometimes I'm afraid to throw away the memory of a date night with Bry, an idea for my next book, the encouraging words of a friend, the evidence of my kids' growing up (school notes, receipts for diapers, etc.). But I'm getting better. I've begun by tossing all the bad to so-so photographs, regularly cleaning out my files, and daily adding to my recycling basket.

I'm sharing my obsession with you humbly. And I want to point out that paper products, including the Bible, are not meant to be idolized. Though I enjoy the actual physical weight of the Bible in my lap early in the morning or on my chest as I fall asleep, I realize that it represents (or embodies) more than its paper shell. Its stories require me to trust what I cannot see. Its words encourage me to hold fast to hopes. Its narrative asks me to keep faith, believe in God, and be patient. Interestingly enough, it asks me to think about things I can't presently touch, see, or taste.

Still, I treasure my stack of Bibles, including my first Ryrie and the pale pink New American Standard with my maiden name, Pelinka, inscribed in curly letters. In the same way that Bryan's goodnight kisses remind me of our invisible marriage covenant, so Bibles tangibly remind me of God's love, faithfulness, and presence in my life.

This morning, when I picked up my most recently acquired copy of the Bible, a bright orange New International Version, I enjoyed its smooth leather binding and shocking color. I gently thumbed through its silver-edged pages, enjoying a fingertip tickling. I even held the book to my nose, experiencing olfactory delight as fresh, leather tannins poked my nostrils. In that moment I considered the shape of God's love. *It must look a lot like the circle of Bryan's arms,* I decided. Then I tried to imagine the way God's love might smell. I decided it must be similar to the aroma of freshly printed books mingled with a hint of sawdust.

> *Part of what has nourished my Judeo-Christian faith is,*
> *of course, the Bible, and the Bible is a potent icon*
> *for me.... I grew up with Bible stories in a big book*
> *one of my godparents had given me and which I*
> *read over and over again.*[4]
>
> MADELEINE L'ENGLE

Our Word—*Scriptures, Insights, & Suggestions*

Certain portions of the Bible are truly iconic for me, often the more poetic or the wild and wondrous words in Ezekiel or Daniel or Job. They are open doors to the glory of God, the God who loves and cares for us creatures.[5]

MADELEINE L'ENGLE

1. How do you feel about considering God as your Husband, as described in Isaiah 54:5? Does He seem present, loving, and committed to you? Why or why not?

2. Have you experienced an iconic representation of God's love in a sunset, piece of stained glass, a meal, or meaningful memento? If so, describe the experience. Or make a list of tangible ways God has loved you.

3. Hold your Bible. Feel the weight of it. Leaf through its pages. Hug it to your chest. Perhaps sleep with it under your pillow. Write a journal entry about how these activities make you feel.

A kind of envy possesses me as I think of the disciples. I know that...I have the help of God the Holy Spirit, but to have Jesus as my friend, with skin on, with his voice tones and personal mannerisms and unique, memorable facial features...and then I remember that I do meet Jesus in the flesh as I hear him speaking from the mouths of my friends, as his love wraps 'round in their hugs, their letters, their phone calls, their laughter, their tears.[6]

LUCI SHAW

Heart Scribbles

The Bible as a Love Letter

*Ever since my move to Minnesota, Sally and I have had
to rely on phone calls to keep in touch.
We write letters, too…More often than not, we pick up
the phone and end up spilling our letters before they even
reach their destinations.*[1]

CHERI MUELLER

*Friendship means frequent phone calls, letters,
face-to-face visits—staying in touch.*[2]

LUCI SHAW

Her Word—*Cheri's Letter on an Unlikely Tablet*

Because of Cheri's move to Minnesota, we've accrued astronom-
ical phone bills and titanic travel tabs. During our most recent
budget buster, we partook in an adventure for ourselves and combined brood of six. It began with a gathering at one of Minnesota's
10,000 azure lakes. There the kids got sandy, sunburned, water-
logged, and whiny. Cheri and I got to complete a conversation of
one (or maybe two) sentences at a time.

Later on the trip we chased our kids, who were in turn chasing a handful of bantams and tailless cats around The Wild Rumpus. The Rumpus, a children's bookstore where caged rats live under the floorboards, has a crack-painted ceiling that makes you feel as if you've just walked into the pages of *Chicken Little*. Strangely, even after we left, it seemed like the sky was falling as we struggled to shepherd our six charges back to our minivans.

The next day we squeezed in The Barkus Parade. Along with the kids, we cheered for pet owners and their dogs. They were dressed as literary characters from children's books. During the pageant, we saw five embarrassed pooches done up as Angelina the Ballerina...one lab mix as an alligator, accompanied by his owner, Peter Pan...a poodle adorned in a chaipo playing Mulan...and dozens of other tail-wagging spectacles.

As the ludicrous line marched down a cobblestone sidewalk in front of the library, our kids poked us. "Look, Mama! Lllllooooook! That dog's wearing a wig...a tutu...shoes!"

Another sunset, and Cher and I shared about half a dozen words before singing songs, telling tales, and tucking our six-personed wild rumpus into bed. We stayed up way too late that night finally eking out uninterrupted stories about our love lives, our latest writing endeavors, our disappointments and dreams.

I don't know how we conjured up the energy (maybe it was because we'd finally been emancipated by the elixir of adult conversation), but on the last day of our trip, we took an imaginary vacation to Egypt, including building paper pyramids, eating an Egyptian feast, and writing hieroglyphic messages on paper bags. For that day's dazzling finale, as stars sparkled above our heads and lightning bugs danced about our shoulders, we adorned our kids and ourselves with glow-stick necklaces, earrings, belts, and crowns. Then we danced around Cheri's front yard with tribal fervor to 50s tunes.

I treasure face-to-face visits like these. They create memories as glowing and real and lasting as lightning bugs. I also treasure our e-mail and snail mail connections. There's something unexpectedly magical about receiving written correspondence from Cheri. Over our 20 years of shared friendship, I've saved many of her written connectors. They include thank-you notes, birthday cards, letters, poems, and postcards. Each begins with "Dear Sally," and sandwiched between conversational sentences are word-gems such as...

> WOW! What a year this has been. I pray you will continue to grow in Faith, Hope, and Love...God is good! Happy, Happy Birthday!

> Thank you for being such a special and irreplaceable friend in my life. There will never be anyone who shares the journey quite like you...

> I want you to know you are in my thoughts and prayers this weekend. I know your words will BLESS the women of Blanchard Church...

> Congratulations on the birth of *Play with Me!* You're the best mom, friend, and writer I know—what a joy to celebrate all three of these things in our book! Thanks for inspiring me in life and helping me "grow up" in God!

And her most recent words written to me:

> Thank you for making the trip to see us this summer! It was such a joy to see the kids and to foster our friendship.

Over the years, as we've shared adventures and watched our children grow up, Cher and I have been "growing up" in God too. Her words make me keenly aware of this. In the same way a diary marks a private journey, Cher's letters celebrate our shared journey.

Along the way, her notes have also lifted me like a hot cup of coffee on a cold day out of life's momentary malaises. Through ink on paper, Cher challenges, celebrates, and makes me feel known and loved. When I've been discouraged about my inadequacies as a wife, mother, and writer, Cher cheers me on. I savor her scribbles, reading and rereading them when I need encouragement or companionship.

After our wild and wacky adventure this summer, I realized that Cher herself is a living, breathing letter. When I'm with her I sense a wise, wondrous, sometimes wacky presence. She carries the presence of the Spirit of the living God inside her. Just like Cher writes with ink on Hallmark cards, she has also written on my heart by her very presence.

> *You yourselves are our letter, written on our hearts, known and read by everybody. You show that you are a letter from Christ...written not with ink but with the Spirit of the living God, not on tablets of stone but on tablets of human hearts.*
>
> 2 CORINTHIANS 3:2-3

God's Word—*Embossing Our Hearts*

> *My [daughter] keep my words...within you... Write them on the tablet of your heart.*
>
> PROVERBS 7:1,3

Like Cheri in my life, God walks with us through life. He sits beside us and cheers with us at parades. He laughs at the curious and sometimes bizarre occurrences in our lives. He longs to have meaningful conversations with us and dance with us under the stars in the glow of warm, waning, summer evenings. Wherever we are, God is chasing us around in the wild rumpus.

He also scribbles down His heart in letters, just like Cheri does. These letters of encouragement can be most easily found in the

Bible's letters (epistles) written by Paul. We can read these letters in the same way I read Cheri's letters to me: as personal, poignant, practical connectors.

In addition to spending time with friends in the various churches he helped establish, the apostle Paul wrote many notes of encouragement. According to the *Holman Study Bible,* "The nature of Paul's work made letters an important means of communication. He traveled widely...He spent part of his time imprisoned. He continued and expanded his ministry by writing letters."[3]

Did you know that more than half of the books in the New Testament are letters? I guess God knows that faith-walking people—then and now—need encouragement for their journeys. Paul, with his tinderbox of overzealousness, was the perfect one to spark our hearts. I'm so amazed that God's love letters to the Galatians, Philippians, Ephesians, Colossians, and Corinthians make me feel loved too. Here are some of my favorite heart scribbles from Paul's epistles. As you read them, insert your name in the blanks, sit back, and receive encouragement. Hopefully this eclectic collection will quicken your connection with God.

> See what large letters I use as I write to you with my own hand!...The grace of our Lord Jesus Christ be with your spirit, _____ (Galatians 6:11 and 18).

> For this reason, ever since I heard about your faith in the Lord Jesus and your love for all the [girlfriends], I have not stopped giving thanks for you, remembering you in my prayers. I keep asking that the God of our Lord Jesus Christ...may give _____ the Spirit of wisdom (Ephesians 1:15-17).

> Be imitators of God, _____, therefore, as dearly loved children and live a life of love (Ephesians 5:1-2).

> Whatever you have learned or received or heard from me, or seen in me—put into practice, _____. And the God of peace will be with you (Philippians 4:9).

Though I am absent from you in body, I am present with you in spirit and delight to see...how firm _____'s faith in Christ is (Colossians 2:5).

Let the peace of Christ rule in your hearts...Let the word of Christ dwell in _____ richly as you teach and admonish one another with all wisdom...with gratitude in your hearts to God (Colossians 3:15-16).

We can turn to the Word of God, dwell on it, and reread Paul's scribbles over and over in the same way I reread Cheri's letters. As we do, we'll receive encouragement for our journey, strength for the trip, and a sense of companionship along the way. And we'll realize that the Bible is a love letter written with the lives of those who have gone before us embossed on our hearts.

Our Word—*Scriptures, Insights, & Suggestions*

> *The one good thing about not seeing you
> is that I can write you letters.*
>
> SVETLANA ALLILUYEVA

1. Do you save letters and other written correspondence? If you do, reread some of the old cards, notes, and e-mails. Do they mark rites of passage in your life? Do they give you feelings of encouragement and companionship? Why or why not?

2. Take some time to read one of Paul's epistles this week. Take it in as if it were a note to you from a well-intentioned friend. Notice how the words feel on your tongue and in your mind. What do they mean to you?

3. Sit quietly and handwrite a note of encouragement to a friend.

As you do, imagine the way Paul must have felt as he wrote love letters to encourage the early church.

A letter always seemed to me like immortality because it is the mind alone without corporeal friend.

EMILY DICKINSON

You Can Call Me...

The Bible Giving Names

Once there was a man who was a Namer.
That is what he was called by God, to be, and to do...
The Lord God formed every beast of the field and every
fowl of the air and brought them to Adam to see what
he would name them: and whatever Adam called every
living creature, that was its name.[1]

MADELEINE L'ENGLE

Her Word—*Heather's Nicknames*

Like the biblical Adam, my friend Heather is a prolific namer. In college alone, she labeled me with these nicknames: *Salzy, Salsa, Sals, Sal-Sal, and Pally Selinka* (a Pig Latin amalgam of my first and maiden name). During our senior year at Wheaton College, Heather gave *all* the women with whom we shared a house similarly amalgamated names. And, much to my amusement, she didn't spare herself from the hilarity of curious nomenclature. Heather's personal titles included numerous reconfigurations of her favorite moniker, *The Geek Magnet: Magnet, Mag, Mag-o-my-net, Geek,* and the ever popular *Mag.*

Since our collegiate days, Heather hasn't slacked in bequeathing nicknames. Her children answer to dozens of short and long versions of their given names. They even respond to calls for *Brother* and *Sister* (which Heather, of course, endlessly reconfigures into *Sis, Sissy, Sis-tah*).

Lately Heather's family of four has acquired a multitude of pets. With the naming of each new critter, I've been cracked up to notice how Brother and Sissy have inherited a propensity for creating crazy names from their Mama (*Moms, Momsie, Mamalicious*). Their first naming adventure involved a mayo jar of Sea Monkeys. To my dismay, Heather's kids gave every single smelly, feathery friend the same name: *Swimmy-Bob*.

After 13 days, and a tragic demise, the brine shrimp were replaced by two goldfish: *Goldilocks* and *Porridge*. They lasted mere months before the kids started begging for a puppy.

Trying to stave off the wish for a warm-blooded companion, Heather purchased *Veronica,* the Venus flytrap; *Sampson* and *Delilah,* a pair of box turtles; and *Pepper* and *Sugar,* black and white guinea pigs. ("Why not *Pepper* and *Salt?*" I asked. I got only a shrug in answer.)

When the rodents were sunning in the backyard, they got gobbled by a neighbor's cat. Heather had no choice but to make her kids' dreams of a canine come true. One visit to the animal shelter was all it took. By the third cage, Heather became infatuated with a spotted mutt shaking a round rump and sporting an unavoidable smile.

That very day the dog barreled through Heather's front door into the arms of Brother and Sissy. While the new pet licked the kids and batted their arms with a flailing tail, Sister said, "She's so sweet…and loving."

Brother looked up at Heather, "I know just what to call her: Sweetie Loving!"

Trying to be sensitive to her son, Hannah said, "Honey, this doggy already has a name. It's Samantha."

Samantha licked Sister's cheek. "She doesn't look anything like a Samantha. She's more of a *Sweetie Loving,*" Heather's little girl protested.

Sitting down on the foyer floor, my friend examined the dog. "Let me take a better look," Heather said as the new family member bounced over and flopped into "the Magnet's" lap. "Maybe you two are right. This dog *does* look like a Sweetie Loving."

Punctuating the thought, the dog thumped her tail as if agreeing with the new title. The kids jumped up and down. To this day, that bubble-butted mutt comes running if anyone calls "Sweetie Loving."

I recently got an e-mail from Heather with attached pictures of her kids running through the sprinkler with Sweetie Loving. The note was addressed to *Salzy.* Reading my nickname in the salutation made me grin. It also made me realize that Heather names and renames people and pets in a profound, sweet, and silly way of loving.

> *If you name somebody or something, you discover that the act of Naming is very closely connected with the act of loving, and hating is involved with unNaming—taking a person's name away, causing anyone to be an anonymous digit, annihilating the spirit.*[2]
>
> MADELEINE L'ENGLE

God's Word—*Gifting White Stones*

> *You will be with child and give birth to a son, and you are to give him the name Jesus.*
>
> LUKE 1:31

During a dull, stay-at-home-mom day of laundry, dirty dishes, and even dirtier floors, I turned on *Oprah* in an effort to procrastinate from housework. The program featured Lisa Ling's heart-touching and informative piece about "China's Lost Daughters." As I've mentioned before, I cried half the day after seeing graphic footage of a beautiful, but terminally sick orphan who was left alone to die in a hidden room in one of China's social welfare institutions.

The face of that nymph of a girl is emblazoned in my memory. Her taut, open, trying-to-wail mouth, which had no strength left for sound, haunts me. Her sweet but teary almond eyes still speak to me in dreams. I'll also never forget her name: *Mei Ming*. The name sounds as beautiful as the child. But its meaning is tragic: "No Name." This nameless one was treated as such. Unloved, uncared for, unknown, unwanted, alone without even the dignity of a name.

The only comfort I found that day—and months later when I traveled to a Chinese orphanage and saw dozens of priceless, but nameless ones—was to imagine God having a name for Mei Ming and each of her abandoned sisters. He sees these precious girls, knows them, gives them names of honor like An (Peaceful), Bo (Precious), Hua (Flower).

God is a namer like Adam and Heather. At His command, when an angel announced to Mary that she'd bear a divine child, the message of what to name the baby was also squeezed in. Over and over in Scripture God bestows names. He knows naming is important. That's why, during turning points in His children's lives, God sometimes even *re*-names!

After 99 years of being called Abram, God appeared to the not-so-confident Old Testament leader. With a mere "ha" and an almighty promise, God changed history: "This is my covenant with you: You will be the father of many nations. No longer will you be called Abram; your name will be Abra*ha*m, for I have made you a father of many nations" (Genesis 17:4-5).

After a sleepless night of wrestling with God, Jacob also got a new name: "Your name will no longer be Jacob, but Israel, because you have struggled with God and with men and have overcome" (Genesis 32:28). A similar thing is recorded in the New Testament regarding one of Jesus' friends: Simon. After Simon told the Carpenter from Galilee that he believed his teacher to be God's Son, Jesus said, "Blessed are you, Simon...I tell you that you are Peter, and on this rock I will build my church" (Matthew 16:17-18).

The Bible doesn't stop with stories of God naming His historic heroes. It also gives *us* new names. When reading Scripture, notice how God addresses us. We're regarded as *beloved* (Deuteronomy 33:12), *royal* and *holy* (1 Peter 2:9), *precious* (Psalm 116:15), *beautiful* (Isaiah 52:7), and many more glorious, undeserved, affirming names.

In the book of Revelation, God promises to one day give all of us white stones with new names written upon them (2:17). This gives me goose bumps to imagine each of us being in God's presence, receiving our stones, turning them over and over in our palms, tracing the names engraved on their smooth surfaces. We will all receive surprising names, denoting acceptance, grace, and beauty through Christ!

One of our most valuable titles—in light of Mei Ming's story—is *adopted daughter.* "In love he predestined us to be adopted as his [daughters] through Jesus Christ, in accordance with his pleasure and will" (Ephesians 1:4-5). Like Ming, we can rest in God's love—the kind of love that plans for our adoption, longs for our placement into His family, and offers redemptive life-giving names...names that show us who we truly are.

> *To [her] who overcomes, I will...also give [her] a white stone with a new name written on it, known only to [her] who receives it.*
>
> REVELATION 2:17

Our Word—*Scriptures, Insights, & Suggestions*

> *The name that [God] will give each of us in heaven will also reveal to us what God thought of us when he first made us. It will show how much he loves us and how intimately he has known us all along.*[3]
>
> JOYCE SACKETT

1. Do any of your friends call you by nicknames? What one means the most to you and why? How do your nicknames make you feel?

2. Grab a piece of paper or your journal. Write your full name (or one of your nicknames). Study it. Read it. Ponder it. If you don't know the meaning of your name, look it up.

3. Do you like your name? Does it represent you? Why or why not? Do you know the story behind your naming? If not, take time to find out.

4. If you're at a crossroad in your life, ask God what new name He wants for you. Write it down and meditate on its meaning. Live in the fullness and gift of that name.

5. Imagine being at the end of your life and receiving a white stone with your new name written on it in God's handwriting. What do you think the name will be? Why?

6. Can you think of a time while reading the Bible that you discovered one of God's names for you? What passage were you reading? What was the name?

Perhaps part of our new name is being formed as we live the Christian life on earth. As we use our gifts for God's glory and persevere in spite of our weaknesses, God lets us help him write the stories that our new names will tell.[4]

JOYCE SACKETT

A Theme Runs Through It
God's Word Brings Meaning to Our Lives

Themes are the fundamental and often universal ideas explored in a literary work.[1]

PATRICK GARDNER

Theme exists only when an author has seriously attempted to record life accurately or to reveal some truth about it, or when an author has deliberately introduced as a unifying element some concept or theory of life that the story is meant to illustrate.

Frequently, a story...will have something to say about the nature of all human beings or about their relationship to each other or to the universe.[2]

LAURENCE PERRINE

Her Word—*Personal Professor Brother*

Though my brother, Rob, has basketball and testosterone coursing through his major arteries and veins, he's one of my best "girlfriends." I inevitably include him in my "girl talk" books. Though he scrapes doorways at six foot six inches, he can get down on the rug and play dollies with my one year old. He knows me better than anyone on the planet, and I know him as well as Julia Child knew French cuisine. He's intelligent, thoughtful, and extremely enigmatic. A sports attorney by trade, he spends many a night at Los Angeles' Staples Center. But when he's not courtside, supporting one of his players, he can be found in his library or snuggled beside his bride, Kristin, reading.

I've taken wheelbarrows of books out on "inter-library loan" from his personal library. He owns all of my favorites and more: Kathleen Norris' *Cloister Walk*, John Irving's *A Prayer for Owen Meany*, everything C.S. Lewis wrote, world atlases, theological treatises, Dorothy Sayers' *The Mind of the Maker*. Whether we're visiting each other in Chicago or LA, or just talking on the phone, our conversations are usually pulled, as if in a white-capped current, back to books.

Vivid memories burst from the root of a childhood shared with my brother. He and I rode bikes up and down Mawman Hill, hid chunks of Mom's venison burgers in our napkins, explored the field near our home as if we were John Smith and Pocahontas. Rob was even tolerant enough—or I was big-sister-bossy enough—that he let me dress him up like a girl, introducing him as "Roberta" to babysitters and neighbors.

It may sound crazy, but we feel like kids playing in the field again when we talk about "good reads." We forge through ideas, plots, characters, motifs, and symbols with the same explorer spirits we had when searching for roly-polies under rocks and rotten logs.

Rob is my personal professor, challenging my brain, stretching my cerebellum with new concepts and fresh paradigms. He even has a semineurotic habit that helps in our post-grad dialogues. He often types summaries of books he reads, including his favorite quotes. I benefit from "RobsNotes" when he sends portions per-taining directly to my writing or life. Though Rob usually brings facts, figures, and truths to the table and I counter with metaphor, verisimilitude, and the feminine side, whenever we share we're both enlightened.

Recently when I was in LA, I broke down in tears at my brother's kitchen table. Chronic back pain had been taking its toll on me for several years, and it was particularly encumbering and nefarious during my visit.

He dammed my reservoir of sadness with a question: "When was your pain the worst?"

I sniffled, thought, and answered, "Probably when Kristin and I went to the Getty Art Museum."

Rob put a hand on my sagging shoulder. I looked up into his wide, compassionate eyes of dark-chocolate brown. "That's interesting, Sal. Don't you think?"

Desperate to see where Rob was going, I leaned in and waited for him to continue.

"That's *really* interesting. You experienced your most excruciating pain in the midst of some of the most beautiful things on the globe: Greek and Roman antiquities, works by Rubens, Brueghel, Van Gogh. That's profound! Literal pain in the midst of beauty."

My pain didn't go away with Rob's insight or the Advil he gave me. But in days following, when I experienced stabbing pain like I had that day at The Getty, I remember Rob's words. I also remember the pieces of literature in which we noted the symbiotic relationship between pain and beauty. Though I passionately wish my pain would remit, I'm thankful for a brother who could and would take the time to point out themes in my life the same way he found them in art.

Because of Rob's insight, I thought about the way my back pain (and inability to carry a third child) birthed the glorious redemptive adoption of my daughter. I thought about how the pain had also birthed compassion in my heart toward others who suffer. And I'm beginning to realize how the pain is making me slow down during frenetic days to sit down, pick up good books, and visit with friends.

God's Word—*Illuminating the Themes of Our Lives*

> *If literature is a metaphor for the writer's
> experience, a mirror in which that experience is at
> least partially reflected, it is at the same time a mirror
> in which the reader can also see his or her experience
> reflected in a new and potentially transforming way.
> This is what it is like to search for God in a world where
> cruelty and pain hide God.*[3]
>
> FREDERICK BUECHNER

Just as Rob is good at pointing out patterns in my life, the Bible illuminates themes and universal truths in our lives. Though there are thousands of vivid, study-worthy themes in God's Word, let's explore three of my favorites: *Love Gets the Girl, There Is Freedom Within Boundaries,* and *Beauty Is Often Born of Pain.*

Love Gets the Girl

A not-so-swinging single for almost a decade after graduating from Wheaton College, I gravitated to the theme of God's prince-like love for "His girls." I relished the story of Gomer, found in the book of Hosea. An unfaithful, social pariah—a prostitute—she was beloved of and ultimately wed to Hosea, God's prophet. I, an imperfect woman longing for a husband, read her story over and over. Its theme of loving without cause convinced me that God loved me just as I was. It also solidified my hope that someday God's love would incarnate in the man I'd marry.

Along with reading Gomer's story, I memorized portions of Jeremiah, such as chapter 31, verse 3, which reads: "I have loved you with an everlasting love; I have drawn you with loving-kindness." And Song of Songs 2:16: "My beloved is mine, and I am his" (NASB). Though my longing for a husband was not sated until I met and married Bryan, I found much comfort in knowing God's *agape* love for me. A love that "expresses deep and constant love…of a perfect Being towards entirely unworthy objects."[4] Often, I pondered the theme of unyielding love through the metaphor of Jesus, named Faithful and True, riding on a white horse to come for me (Revelation 19:11). The stories and words helped me feel wrapped in love during a stark and lonely wintry season.

Freedom Within Boundaries

Another biblical theme especially vibrant during my single years was freedom through boundaries. I picture this theme undulating through the New Testament like an endless ribbon waving in the wind. It liberates itself from the pages, creating a safe circle in a plush green pasture where God's children run, cartwheel, and rest.

The boundaries are not rigid, unforgiving traffic signals. Instead, they're flexible like a spirit: giving, guiding, protecting. For me during my singleness, one of the boundary lines meant remaining sexually pure until marriage. This did not mean living a prudish, puritanical, nonsensual, passionless life where I couldn't enjoy wearing a lacy dress or savoring a succulent strawberry. It did mean saving one of life's most sensual experiences for my marital mattress.

The freedom in this decision was found in simple moments like the ends of dates when I didn't have to awkwardly worry about extending an invitation to my bedroom or not. It was found in the sweetness of holding hands and first kisses. It lingered in anticipating the holy, hot, giggly, glorious night I'd one day share with my husband. I love that Paul writes, "It is for freedom that Christ has set us free" and "You…were called to be free" (Galatians 5:1 and 13). Thanks be to God for the biblical theme of freedom through boundaries!

Beauty Born of Pain

These days, having given birth to two large sons, I understand firsthand the biblical theme about beauty born of pain. Even John acknowledges, "A woman giving birth to a child has pain because her time has come; but when her baby is born she forgets the anguish because of her joy that a child is born into the world" (John 16:21). It seems that so many times in life pain is the birth canal for things alive with beauty. A seed dies and goes into the ground before it's sprung afresh as a flower (1 Corinthians 15:36-38). The caterpillar and tadpole "die" before their metamorphosis casts aside seedy shells for more grandiose beings. (Sometimes I wonder if it hurts the tadpole to lose his tail and sprout legs. Such transformative beauty must be born of pain.)

The other night when I put my five-year-old Ben to bed, he said, "Mama, my legs are aching." I looked at his gangly, boyish build—appendages like a daddy longleg's—and imagined the man he was becoming before my eyes. "I think you're having growing pains, Ben," I comforted as I dotted his forehead with a kiss.

The hard work of raising children, writing books, making a living, staying physically fit, being intimate can all be painful. But pain is worth the resultant beauty. God moves in mysterious ways, always redeeming, bringing growth and good things from achings. Though God "wounds" us sometimes in order to heal, He is not masochistic. He's our God who asked His Son to die to birth something lovely—to allow us to fully commune with Him again (1 Thessalonians 5:10). Using the pain in our lives, our friends, and His Word, He tenderizes our hearts.

> *If God's goodness is inconsistent with hurting us,*
> *then either God is not good or there is no God: for in the*
> *only life we know He hurts us beyond our worst fears*
> *and beyond all we can imagine…Sometimes it is hard*
> *not to say, "God forgive God."…But if our faith is true,*
> *He didn't. He crucified Him.*[5]
>
> C.S. Lewis

Our Word—*Scriptures, Insights, & Suggestions*

1. Do you have a friend who is able to identify themes in your life? If not, ask someone close to your heart if he or she notices any. Do you see recurrent themes in your life? What are they? Take a walk and think about your personal themes. Write sentence summaries of them.

2. Have you experienced the kind of love God had for Gomer? Freedom through boundaries or the way pain births beauty? Invite a friend over for coffee or tea and talk about these themes.

3. What biblical themes deeply resonate with you? Why? List biblical and literary references such as Anne Lamott's "God isn't there to take away our suffering or our pain but to fill it with his or her presence"[6] and Isaiah 61:1 and 3, "The Spirit of the Sovereign LORD is on me, because the LORD has anointed me...to bestow on them a crown of beauty instead of ashes, the oil of gladness instead of mourning, and a garment of praise instead of a spirit of despair" to support these themes.

I also read the Bible stories for comfort...
I took my grief to the Bible for healing. I cannot think of
any human grief that is not expressed for us in the Bible,
from the very beginning stories in Genesis.[7]

MADELEINE L'ENGLE

Great Physicians
God's Word Heals

When do we receive real comfort and consolation?
Is it when someone teaches us how to think or act? Is it
when we receive advice about where to go or what to do?
Is it when we hear words of reassurance and hope?
Sometimes, perhaps. But what really counts is that in
moments of pain and suffering someone stays with us.
More important than any particular action or word of
advice is the simple presence of someone who cares.[1]

HENRI NOUWEN

Her Word—*Kristin, a Pediatrician with Nail Polish*

My brother's wife, Kristin, has recently completed an arduous medical school residency in pediatrics. She survived puzzling patient sicknesses, emergent injuries, and inhumane hours. Last night, with pride, tears, and bright-blue tissue paper, I wrapped two books about the life of Mother Teresa for Kristin. On the title page of one of the books, I wrote:

Dearest Kristin,

We want to celebrate your completion of medical school and congratulate you on earning The Resident of the Year Award!

To honor you and mark this moment, we thought it appropriate to gift you with two books about Mother Teresa. Like you, she built her home where suffering lived. She dressed in compassion. She knew that "God is our God, the God of the living. In his divine womb life is always born again. The great mystery is not the cures, but the infinite compassion which is their source" (Henri Nouwen).

As a pediatrician, you will surely cure many sick children. At the same time, you'll probably watch others suffer and die. Your gift to all of these patients will be your deep, rapid, and river-wide compassion. It's a quality we noticed in you when we first met you. You have a servant's heart for others...really, for the world. May God bless you as you bring your well-earned medical knowledge and heart of compassion to many children and their families.

With pride and joy in your accomplishments,

Bry, Sal, Ben, Ayden, and Emily

For the last few years, I've relished Kristin's residency stories. I feel as if I were there the day she donned yucky-green scrubs and brought baskets of nail polish, makeup, and *Glamour* magazines to a pediatric cancer ward. I can perfectly imagine the time she put down her prescription pad and cried with the mother and father whose toddler was pronounced DOA after choking on an almond found beneath the family room sofa.

Another story I'll never forget involved an expectant couple who received fetal tests indicating their baby would be born severely deformed and with little to no cognitive ability. Kristin listened to the parents' concerns, worries, fears, devastation, even anger. When they decided to see the pregnancy to full-term, Kristin enthusiastically supported their decision. Nine months later, when the baby was born with a loud wail and impeccable health, Kristin joined in an exuberant neonatal celebration.

Regardless of the results of Kristin's medical treatments and recommendations, she's committed to *being with her patients* and their parents. She understands that compassion means being *with* (com) people in their *moment of pain* (passion). In rooms smelling of stagnant air and medicine, standing beside beds tucked tightly in sterile sheets, Kristin accompanies the hurting as they face a melee of diagnoses, symptoms, and options. Her eyes, gentle and emerald-green with concern, *really* see the patients whom she serves. Her voice, never calculating or cold, sounds like the cautionary melody of a mother bird singing to the birdies in her nest.

It's not surprising that my altruistic sister-in-law even plans her vacations around helping those in need. Dr. Kristin frequently totes black bag, stethoscope, and medical skills to Africa where she treats AIDS orphans or to India where she recently sojourned to broaden her medical knowledge. In her first "real" job as a doctor, she expressed pure glee when she discovered her medical responsibilities included pro-bono work at a local crisis pregnancy center. There she gives postnatal care to babies in uniquely difficult or precarious family situations. Kristin almost did a cartwheel when she discovered that her medical group is also involved in an annual mission to Africa.

Recently I visited Kristin and Rob in Los Angeles. I was impressed by their artful, comfortable décor, which was executed in shades of chocolate brown and cream. Their art, furniture, and floral arrangements took my breath away. Though Kristin and Rob have built an exquisite place in LA, Kristin's true home is any place where people are sick and suffering.

> *Compassion means going directly to*
> *those people and places where suffering is most acute*
> *and building a home there.*[2]
>
> HENRI NOUWEN

> *We are all created with the ability, the need to reach out,
> to join ourselves with others, in love, to feel with and for
> others. The words* sym-pathy *(with passion) and* em-pathy
> *(in passion) both tell a story.*[3]

LUCI SHAW

God's Word—*Healing in the Pages*

> *God's compassion is total, absolute, unconditional,
> without reservation. It is the compassion of the one who
> keeps going to the most forgotten corners of the world,
> and who cannot rest as long as he knows that there are
> still human beings with tears in their eyes.*[4]

HENRI NOUWEN

The Bible, in both Old and New Testaments, tells us graphically about God's compassion. *Splangchnizomai,* the Greek word meaning "to be moved with compassion" is found 12 times in the New Testament. It connotes a "spilling of guts," indicating that when Jesus was feeling compassion it came from a deep, central place within Him. In essence, a compassionate spirit is Christ's essence. And it literally moved Him from heaven to earth.

When I think of compassion, I immediately remember Jesus' Passion. I remember the day He walked the Via Dolorosa (The Way of Suffering). And I think of the man named Simon, a Cyrene, who was forced to carry the cross for part of the journey on that Jerusalem road. In all four gospels Simon is merely briefly mentioned. But I like to imagine that he was a follower of Jesus. I see the way he trailed after Jesus, bearing the heavy, splintering cross piece. I imagine that as Simon dragged the cross behind a dehydrated, whip-striped Jesus he was portraying the world's truest sense of *com*passion—actually being *with* Jesus during the arche-typal passion. The Bible doesn't elaborate, but I like to think Simon had encouraging words for Jesus.

I can just hear Simon whispering to a battered, bruised, bloody, bedraggled Christ, "You can do it. We're almost there." Maybe Simon was once in the midst of one of the crowds that followed Jesus? Perhaps he even borrowed some of Jesus' own words to comfort Him: "Blessed are the poor in spirit, for theirs is the kingdom of heaven...Blessed are those who hunger and thirst for righteousness, for they will be filled...Blessed are those who are persecuted because of righteousness, for theirs is the kingdom of heaven. Blessed are you when people insult you, persecute you and falsely say all kinds of evil against you...Rejoice and be glad, because great is your reward in heaven" (Matthew 5:3,6,10-12).

Christ made His home in first-century Palestine: eating, walking, speaking, befriending, dying. Simon the Cyrene made his home near the One who had come by carrying the cross, wailing with Christ, caring.

Many of my friends have been Simon to me. And when they cannot be next to me, the Bible is my Simon, walking with me, whispering words of encouragement when my days feel dark and dismal. When I'm suffering, I also turn to the story of the "Woman of Bleeding" in Luke 8. She wrestled through the crowd to get near to Jesus, and with last-ditch need and hope, reached for the hem of His robe. In His presence, she was healed. Near Him, touching Him with faith, close enough to hear His voice, she was healed.

One of my dearest friends, who sometimes struggles with depression, asks her husband to read Scripture aloud to her on particularly dark days. Because of my own chronic back pain that sometimes prohibits me from reading or praying, I think her idea is brilliant. She says that when she's unable to read the Bible, hearing God's Word read in her husband's resonant bass calms her and makes her more aware of truth and light and God's presence.

Words can be healing. It amazes me how opening the Bible to

certain passages spreads a healing balm on broken bodies, hearts, and spirits. Whether we reach for the hem of Jesus ourselves or a friend does it for us, the truth of God-with-us, God as our true Home, helps.

In the Bible God promises to be our Healer. He never promises a cure. But He promises, like Kristin, to see our pain and be with us in it. No matter how chronic our hurt or how deep our depression, our Healer is waiting with a surprising, mysterious, ultimate healing. He is making His home with us. We may not understand this in the middle of the muck and mire of our circumstances. The cancer may not be remitted, depression may not always be assuaged, babies may die too soon. But God will ultimately redeem, renew, restore. When we need help believing this, reading the Bible (or having someone read it to us) can bring us closer to Jesus, near enough to touch the hem of His garment.

A woman was there who had been subject to bleeding for twelve years, but no one could heal her.
She came up behind him and touched the edge of his cloak, and immediately her bleeding stopped.

Luke 8:43-44

I am the LORD, who heals you.

Exodus 15:26

Our Word—*Scriptures, Insights, & Suggestions*

1. Is there a wound in your life that needs healing? Have you considered how God's Word can be a salve for your wound? Take a walk and let God's wisdom wash over you. Journal your thoughts and His reply.

2. Some of my favorite healing passages are Exodus 15:26; Isaiah 53:5; Malachi 4:2; Luke 8:40-56; 2 Corinthians 12:1-10; 1 Peter 2:24. When you have time, read a few...or have a friend read them to you.

3. The psalms can be particularly healing. Try using the "one's place," mathematically speaking, in today's date and reading the corresponding psalms. (For example, if today is the fifteenth, read Psalm 5, 15, 25, 35, 45, etc.).

4. Do you feel God is your Home, your Healing Room? Why or why not? Ask Him to give you healing, hope, and help through the Bible.

5. Consider practical ways of making your "home" or "place" near someone who needs healing (i.e., volunteer at a food pantry, sing carols at a nursing home, take a mission trip, pray with a hurting friend, open a spare room to someone who needs a place to stay, prepare a meal for a family dealing with chronic illness).

> *God comes where there is pain and brokenness,*
> *waiting to heal, even if the healing*
> *is not the physical one we hope for.*[5]
>
> MADELEINE L'ENGLE

8

Frequent Flyers

*The Bible Takes
Us on a Journey*

*There is another sort of traveling and another sort of
reading. You can eat the local food and drink the local
wines, you can share the foreign life, you can begin to see
the foreign country as it looks, not to the tourist, but to its
inhabitants. You can come home modified, thinking and
feeling as you did not think and feel before.*[1]

C.S. LEWIS

Her Word—*Tina's Ticket*

For a few years Tina and I were in a Bible study together. We shared prayers for healing, life stories, and dozens of piping hot cups of java. I can't even guess the number of times she prayed for my back to stop aching or the times she comforted me during moments of sorrow regarding the fact that I couldn't carry a third child.

When Bryan and I announced to the group that we'd be adopting a little girl from China, Tina was thrilled. The mother of a darling little lady herself, Tina passed on lacy, pink hand-me-downs and prepared me for "sugar and spice and everything nice." Near the end of our adoptive journey, after months of a "paper pregnancy" and the accompanying exorbitant adoption costs, Bryan and I were depleted. Emotionally tired of waiting and financially stretched, we were getting ready to tap into resources such as a home equity loan to complete the adoption process. Though we had been graciously helped by family, friends, and a philanthropic organization, we still had to come up with one last, very large payment for airfare.

I'll never forget the night Tina, her husband, Ken, Bryan, and I stood by a roaring fountain in our neighborhood mall. We had just dined on mall food—pizza to be exact—and lots of laughter. The kids had a few pennies and wishes to throw into the fountain while the adults chatted. Mid-conversation Tina said, "Ken and I would like to get your tickets to China for you."

Immediately tears began to spring from my eyes like the fountain we watched. With ineffable wells of gratitude, Bry and I hugged our dear friends. As we did, we knew that no expression of thanks—hugs, cards, or gifts from China—would adequately express the way their abundant generosity brought fresh breath to our lives.

On the plane November 16, I felt the most thankfulness I've ever experienced. I cross-stitched and repeatedly gazed into Bryan's blues as he listened to music, paged through a *Consumer Reports* and watched *The Shawshank Redemption*.

I was mesmerized by the map function of the tiny screen mounted into the back of the chair in front of me. It pictured various views of the globe and our traveling plane. The first shot was an animated look at our plane, a B777, flying from Chicago and heading directly north. *Because of Tina and Ken, we're on this plane!* I thought.

Within moments, we were over Wisconsin, then Minnesota, then Canada. Five hours and a few hundred cross-stitches into the flight the view changed. We were looking with a bird's-eye view directly down at the North Pole. The world looked strange from this perspective. Chicago to the east, New York north, Beijing west, Los Angeles south, Belhi, Baghada, Moscow to the northwest, and

London way north. As we flew, the screen showed a red thread marking our path. It trailed like a kite's long, lovely tail.

I thought of the Chinese proverb, "An invisible red thread connects those who are destined to meet." I thought about the way we were connected to Ken and Tina, to our boys, to the little girl waiting in JiangXi. I pondered the way we are *all* connected by the red thread of God's love.

Outside our window the sun was setting in a thin, reddish-orange rim. Back on the miniature screen, I noticed the tip of our plane's animated wing touching the map's dot representing the North Pole. It was 6:30 PM (Chicago time). According to the screen, we were at an altitude of 35,000 feet, flying at 568 MPH, the atmosphere was -68 degrees, and we had traveled 3,394 miles... with 3,300 miles to go before arriving in Beijing. "The flight is going so fast," I commented to Bry. He agreed.

The flight attendant brought our second (of three) mini-meals. It was Chinese noodles served with United Airline chopsticks and an almond cookie. I began to cry because the cuisine made me realize how physically close we were to our "Little Ling Ladybug," but we still had days to wait before holding her in our arms.

We arrived in Beijing, checked into our hotel, contacted the adoption people, and settled in for the complicated process. During our free time we touched silk and purchased pearls for the baby. On Shamian Island we walked a homeopathic street of healing where vendors sold dried sea horses, snake wine, live scorpions, tiger paws, and starfish. We were also welcomed into a tiny native home in the labyrinth of a Hutong village.

Because of Tina and Ken's generosity with the tickets, we were able to take in the culture of China, taste Peking duck, smell air from the heights of the Great Wall, and touch intricate copper curlings of cloisonné. We fell in love with our little girl's homeland. We memorialized the journey in photographs that will be part of our daughter's red thread.

The red thread of Tina and Ken's love introduced us to many

warm, welcoming people: a smiling waitress at the Gloria Plaza Hotel, who taught me a new Chinese word (*punyo,* friend) and gave me a pink pearl from her hometown; maternal, compassionate, caring social workers at the Chinese welfare institutions; dozens of curious citizens in Southern China who thought my tall, blond husband must be a superstar basketball player; and, ultimately, a beautiful, long eye-lashed little girl.

On our flight home, Tina managed to book us a middle spot with two extra seats. With Bry on one side and me on the other, Emily slept on the two seats between most of the way home. Exhausted from travel and dozens of sleepless nights with our new baby, we couldn't believe where Tina and Ken's tickets had taken us. Even though I read every book I could get my hands on about China, nothing could have prepared me for this trip Bry and I were able to take because of our friends' help. Because of their gift, my new lullaby is not *Jesus Loves Me,* but *Jesu Ai Ni.* I sing it often, embracing the Chinese language, my new home away from home, and a long-awaited daughter.

God's Word—*Ticket to the Journey of a Lifetime*

You can go beyond the first impression that a [book] makes on your modern sensibility. By study of things outside [literature], by comparing it with other [works], by steeping yourself in the vanished period, you can then re-enter the [book] with eyes more like those of the natives; now perhaps seeing that the associations you gave to the old words were false, that the real implications were different than you supposed.[2]

C.S. Lewis

The Bible takes us to places and introduces us to people we'd never experience on our own: the beginning of time, a desert boat builder, a whale inhabiter, first-century Palestine, a stable in Bethlehem, the mind of the Maker, beachside picnics with stinky fishermen, the golden streets of God's kingdom, Jesus' heart. Sometimes when we read the Bible, it can feel a lot like it did for me when Tina and Ken provided the tickets for a China-bound 777 and I looked at the animated map. The Bible lifts us out of our ordinary life and gives us a variety of fresh, paradigm-shifting views of the globe, of history, of our own travelings. After reading a few chapters—taking a virtual vacation, if you will—we return to our daily lives enriched, broadened, with vivified perspectives and hopes.

When I think of the sojourns I've taken because of my ticket—the Bible—I have a few favorites. Time and again I've gone to a small Samarian town called Sychar. Jesus and his friends are walking from Judea to Galilee. The disciples go to buy food and Jesus meets a woman—a *Samaritan* woman (John 4).

The woman, whom I'll call Nancy, is drawing water at a famous well…the well of Sychar, literally the "well of falsehood." (The well and town earned their name from Jacob, Isaac and Rebekah's son, who cheated his twin brother, Esau, out of his birthright. Jacob still wound up being the father of the twelve tribes of Israel.) As Nancy's story continues we see that Jacob's deception isn't the only mendacity connected with the well.

Picture this. Jesus' friends have just finished baptizing a slew of disciples in Judea. Proudly they walk through Samaria, shoulders back, giving high fives to Jesus and each other. They notice a well in the distance. Their enthusiasm buzzes more rapidly with hope of cold, clear water and a meal in the nearby downtown.

The twelve head toward the main drag to grab fish and chips while Jesus rests His weary, blistered feet at the well. Not long after He sits down, Nancy comes with her water jar.

She tries to avoid Jesus' look, but He grabs her darting, dark-brown eyes with His gentle stare. "Will you give me a drink?" He asks.

Her eyes dart more rapidly. She kicks a clump of crab grass and emancipates a puff of sand. "You are a Jew and I am a *Samaritan woman*." Nancy emphasizes *Samaritan*, knowing Jews despised her and her ilk because of their mixed heritage. She emphasizes *woman* because women in her day are denigrated. "How can you ask me for a drink?" she responds.

The conversation continues—a soul-quenching foray in a dry and weary land. Jesus tells her that though He's asking her for water, He could actually provide "living water" which, if she drinks, will be an eternal thirst quencher. Nancy is completely confused. She has never heard of this magical kind of water. Besides, and probably more importantly, Nancy notices that Jesus doesn't even have a gourd or cup with which to draw water from the well.

The exchange must have been intriguing, electric, mesmerizing. As Nancy steps out on the ledge of belief and asks for the mystical, thirst-quenching drink, Jesus reveals He knows her better than she could imagine. "Sir, give me this water so that I won't get thirsty and have to keep coming here to draw water," she requests.

"Go, call your husband and come back," Jesus replies.

Nancy flushes with shame, trying to hide pain and a sticky personal situation. "I have no husband," she admits.

With compassion and truth burning in His eyes, Jesus notes, "You are right when you say you have no husband. The fact is, you have had five husbands, and the man you now have is not your husband. What you have just said is quite true."

Nancy sets her precious water jar on the precarious edge of the well and takes two steps back. *How does this man see and know me so well? He must be some kind of prophet. Or...could He be the Messiah whom I have heard much about?*

Noticing her confusion and probably knowing her exact thoughts, Jesus continues, "A time is coming when you will worship the Father neither on this mountain nor in Jerusalem...A time is coming and has now come when the true worshipers will worship the Father in spirit and truth."

As Jesus says "truth," Nancy feels a tingling in her heart. Before she knows what she is saying, she blurts, "'I know that Messiah' (called Christ) 'is coming. When he comes, he will explain everything to us.'"

Jesus takes two steps toward Nancy and declares, "I who speak to you am he."

Shocked, excited beyond belief, with a mind swirling with questions, Nancy can't believe whom she's encountered during this trip to the well. She puts her hands to her mouth and falls to her knees.

Bursting the buoyant moment, the disciples return with a ruckus. Nancy, still holding her hands over her mouth, gets up from the ground and goes back to town, saying to the people, "Come, see a man who told me everything I ever did. Could this be the Christ?"

In essence, the woman at the well becomes a lot like Tina is to me, someone who invites others to experience the journey of a lifetime. She leaves her own jar at the well and rushes to tell friends and family about the wonders of encountering Christ.

Whether our tickets take us to the well of Sychar, Chicago, Rome, or Beijing, the traveling is always worth it. Whether we go from burning bush and Red Sea crossing to the wilderness and the Promised Land or from Bethlehem's star and beachfront fires to Gethsemane's hill and a garden's empty tomb, our journeys—our soul-making trips—are so similar. Whether in a plane or through the pages of the Bible, we can travel into the well-like depths of faraway places. When we come home we'll be carrying living treasures that change our lives forever.

Our Word—*Scriptures, Insights, & Suggestions*

1. Are you a traveler? If so, what was your most exotic, nostalgic, meaningful, or favorite trip? Why? What did you take home with you from the trip (souvenirs and life lessons)?

2. What's the most memorable place you've figuratively sojourned

via the Bible? Why is this journey important to you? Share your thoughts and feelings with a friend or write about them.

3. Read John, chapter 4 when you have some free time. How do you feel about Jesus' journey through Samaria? How is His life changed by meeting the Samaritan woman? How is her life changed? How would your life be changed by journeying with them?

4. Have you ever received a life-changing ticket? Remember the journey and thank the ticket giver!

> *It's all about changing what's handed to you, about poking around a little, lifting the corners [of our universe], seeing what's underneath, poking that. Sometimes things work out, sometimes they don't, but at least you're exploring. And life is always more interesting that way.*[3]
>
> ANN M. MARTIN

Family Ties

God's Word Offers Inclusion

> *Growing up Asian in a mainly Caucasian*
> *community was not a miserable and gloomy existence…*
> *It was this constant whirling of East and West that spun*
> *the threads of my identity. At the time I felt these*
> *different threads twisted my life into knots. Now I know*
> *that the fabric of my life is richer for them.*[1]

GRACE LIN

Her Word—*Uncle Gus' Red Envelopes*

One of my favorite people on the planet is Uncle Gus, the husband of my mom's sister, Caryn. With dark, smooth hair, skin the lovely color of a latte, and smiling almond eyes, he is at once handsome, welcoming, and jovial. His Chinese and Filipino roots have mingled wonderfully. Seeing him induces a soul deep "Aloha!" from me, which isn't surprising as he and Caryn live on Kauai. (I just hope he'll forgive me for including him in a *Her Word* section!)

Childhood memories of Uncle Gus are as bold and resonant as his laugh. I vividly remember him at family gatherings at Grandma's rolling ranch in Minnesota. Each morning I'd find him clad in a blue-striped terry robe inevitably eating leftover dinner rice for breakfast (often right out of the serving bowl). Though slim, his ability to eat large quantities of food earned him the nickname "The Chunk." As a young girl I thought the moniker inexorably funny.

Uncle Gus took pity on me—the only girl cousin in a brood of boys. He often defended me from the "Little Devils" (Robby, Jimmy, and Jonny, my brother, and two cousins), taking me on trips to the seminary where he worked or into town on errands. One summer he taught me an entire repertoire of new songs that we performed, accompanied by his guitar, for the entire family. He even gave me a special T-shirt for the occasion. I felt like a super-star. I'll never forget that night and the energy he expended to make me feel like an important part of a family in which I was the butterfly amid a bunch of bullfrogs.

History has a way of repeating itself. Now my sweet little adopted daughter from China finds herself trying to fit into a family full of boys. She also finds herself trying to sort out Chinese roots after being grafted into a predominately Caucasian family tree. Uncle Gus is helping. With the same hands that cradled me, he cradles her. With the same voice that taught me to sing, he sings to her. With the same love, and grace, and honor he includes her and identifies with her from a deep Chinese heritage.

When Bry and I told Uncle Gus we were adopting, he sent us a beautiful Christmas card. It was adorned with cardinals dancing in snow-covered pines and read:

Aloha Sally and Bryan,

When my siblings and I were kids, we always looked forward to receiving our Chinese "Good Fortune" gift from my mom. Tradition required the gift to be wrapped in red paper with a special coin or bill as a token wish for health, long life, and great wealth.

Auntie Caryn and I are happy to continue the tradition with your family now that you are part of the old legacy of Chinese culture.

Merry Christmas!

Love and Hugs,

Uncle Gus

Tucked inside the card was a shiny red envelope that held a silver dollar. Once again "The Chunk" embraced, included, welcomed with aloha-love! Because of him, our daughter feels more deeply linked to our family. And so do I. Our family circle has widened more than I ever could've imagined because of Uncle Gus.

On a recent trip to Chinatown I was standing in line to purchase some soaps. A man behind me heard me using limited Chinese with the clerk and asked if I were Chinese. I thought of my uncle, looked directly into the stranger's eyes, and confidently said, "Yes!" Thanks to Uncle Gus…and now Emily, I've been grafted into the Chinese community. In my heart I'm Chinese.

An invisible red thread connects those who are destined to meet, regardless of time, place, or circumstance. The thread may stretch or tangle, but it will never break.

CHINESE PROVERB

Jesus said, "Whoever welcomes a little child in my name welcomes me."

MATTHEW 18:5

God's Word—*Tie a Red Thread 'Round the Family Tree*

> *Judaism and Christianity have something to do with each other. Judaism and Christianity make a path. They make a path through the Bible, and through history.*[2]
>
> LAUREN WINNER

Just like Uncle Gus, the Bible is about making connections and enlarging family circles—about inclusion. There's a red thread running through the Bible. This red thread is the blood of Christ shed for us, offering hope, a fresh start, a sense of belonging. This thread links Jews and Gentiles, law and grace, Old and New Testaments, history and today. It connects, stitches together, broadens the cloth of God's family.

Reading the Bible, especially the Old Testament, with its Jewish roots can make us feel excluded. Scripture was written primarily by Jewish men. It's filled with stories about Israel, promises for Israel, provisions for Israel, and laws for Israel. Israel is God's chosen nation, a people beloved by Him (Deuteronomy 10:15; Exodus 19:6). And, tantamount to that, Jesus was Jewish.

The Good News of the Bible is that its red thread doesn't end at the Red Sea. If we follow the thread, as foretold by the prophets and foreshadowed in Old Testament narratives, we see it creating a continuous tapestry via the needle of the Divine Artist, moving into the New Testament. And, surprisingly, it continues beyond the pages of God's Book—through space and time—including anyone who desires to be tied into the family of God. "But now in Christ Jesus you who once were far away have been brought near through the blood of Christ" (Ephesians 2:13).

Just as Uncle Gus let me see my Chinese heart, the Bible reveals that *all* of Christendom has Jewish roots. God's grace unites people and makes unpredictable family ties. His New Testament family is the quintessential blended family: an unlikely combination of Jews and Gentiles. "This mystery is that through the gospel the Gentiles are heirs together with Israel, members together of one body, and sharers together in the promise in Christ Jesus" (Ephesians 3:6).

Today God continues to weave all the children of the world together. I can't wait to walk the streets of heaven and see the diversity and surprising familial links woven together by the thread of God's love. Iranians and Pakistanis will embrace. Americans and Kurds will hold hands. Wolves and lambs will live together (Isaiah 11:6). And we'll all be one shockingly happy, unexpected, multicultural family!

I wasn't surprised when I recently heard the ancient Chinese proverb about a connective red thread. The proverb says that those destined to meet are bound by a red thread that stretches but never breaks. God, the author of *all* knowledge, is the source of that wise, ancient Chinese saying. It foretells the way all of God's children are bound together in holy kinship.

Uncle Gus tied Emily and me more tightly into our family. The Bible makes it clear that Christ creates God's children out of foreigners and aliens. He obliterates dividing walls, makes peace, and collects wandering strangers into an enormous family circle (Ephesians 2:11-22). It doesn't matter if we're Chinese or Caucasian, male or female, rich or poor. We can all be grafted into God's family tree woven with His red thread of redemption.

> *You were slain, and with your blood you purchased men for God from every tribe and language and people and nation.*
>
> REVELATION 5:9

Our Word—*Scriptures, Insights, & Suggestions*

> *If the part of the dough offered as first fruits is holy,*
> *then the whole batch is holy; if the root is holy,*
> *so are the branches.*
>
> ROMANS 11:16

1. What are your familial roots? How have they affected, enriched, and deepened your faith?

2. When you imagine the family of God, what do we look like? How have we grafted each other in? How can we be co-weavers of the red thread God began knitting with His words? Why not take up knitting and think about it as your needles click an inspiring rhythm?

3. When you have time to study, read the following passages and trace the red thread through Scripture: Genesis 9:6; Exodus 12:13; 24:8; Leviticus 17:11; Ephesians 1:7; Hebrews 9:22; Revelation 5:9. You may also want to use your concordance to do a word study on *blood, red, crimson,* and *scarlet.* Journal about what you discover.

> *In days to come Jacob will take root, Israel will bud and*
> *blossom and fill all the world with fruit.*
>
> ISAIAH 27:6

10

Red Reminders
Life-Changing Symbols

*We tend to forget, I think, the power of
a symbol to mediate grace.*[1]

SUE MONK KIDD

Her Word—*Cheri's Cardinal Gift*

Cardinals have always been winged reminders of God's grace in
my life. In the midst of disappointments such as rejection letters,
relational fallouts, and the plain old drudgery of daily living, they
show up. Singing in a tree beside my bedroom window, swooping
in front of my car, perched in a bush on my walking path, these
birds are laced into my life like bright-red hope ribbons.

A few years ago when I was struggling to get two of my manuscripts published, every time I thought or prayed for my words to
be validated through publication and touch the lives of others, two
cardinals would cross my path.

As I shared this with Cheri, I worried she'd think I was nuts or
that my bird sightings were mere coincidence, scientifically linked
to the cardinal population and flight patterns in suburban Chicago
land. Instead she told me that when her father was struggling with
cancer, her mother often saw blue jays, which, over time, began to
represent promises of healing. Cheri went on to say that she believes

God uses nature to communicate with us. She even thought she'd heard of a children's book titled *The Ministry of the Birds*.

It touched me to think God sent cardinals to me when I was doubting and discouraged, and He sent blue jays to my friend's mom during a time of illness. My heart moved when Cheri followed our phone conversation with this poem:

> *Two birds, flushed red, side by side fly*
>
> *A promise given that your words too*
>
> *Will be bound, together—*
>
> *Showing others how to soar in the beauty*
>
> *Of a Son-filled sky,*
>
> *Dipped in the gift of crimson-covered friendship*

That night, I sat in my writing room and, in what has now become a tradition, wrote a companion poem to Cheri's:

The Birds

> *A lighting promise on a branch*
> *That brings hope to the soul,*
>
> *When fear and doubt have muted faith*
> *A song of God's control.*
>
> *The dove returned to Noah's ark*
> *Two cardinals wing the words,*
> *Of hope and bluejays wing of health*
>
> *Ministry of the birds.*

A few years ago when Cheri and I were fledgling writers, we were going to travel to Los Angeles to attend our first National Book Expo. At my home before we left, Cheri handed me a small, square box wrapped in red. I opened it to find an adorable wood carving of a baby cardinal. He had tiny brown claws, a tiny beak, two tiny wings timidly reaching out to flap, and two tiny, wondrous black eyes. I put him on my writing desk, a red reminder of the ways God wings healing, hope, protection, help, love, and other crimson-colored graces into our lives.

God's Word—*A Red Thread*

> *We have redemption through his blood.*
>
> EPHESIANS 1:7

Blood. It preserves life. We need it. We can give it. It's a red, redemptive symbol just like my cardinals. I can't help but be reminded of the red thread of Christ's blood that's stitched through the Old and New Testaments when I think of the cardinals that connect my days. In the same way my feathered friends show up day after day—unexpectedly, perfectly placed, singing *Amazing Grace*—so Christ's blood appears on page after page of Scripture and in our lives.

It's easy to think of the shed blood of Christ as a New Testament/New Covenant thing. But God set up blood as important from the get-go. In Genesis 5, the first brother sheds his sibling's blood. Then, in Genesis 9:5-6, God says, "For your lifeblood I will surely demand an accounting...And from each man, too, I will demand an accounting for the life of his fellow man. 'Whoever sheds the blood of man, by man shall his blood be shed; for in the image of God has God made man.'"

Later, in Exodus 12, we see blood's redemptive role when it's slathered on the front doors of Hebrew homes to preserve the lives of baby boys. And in Exodus 24, we see Moses sprinkling the blood of sacrificed young bulls on the people to mark their covenant with God.

All through Old Testament history, God's people were aware of the importance of blood. The iodine smell of it, the staining of it, the warm, thick feel of it surrounded them. And if its presence at the temple altar and slaughterhouses weren't enough, God clarified the symbolic meaning of blood, "For the life of a creature is in the blood, and I have given it to you to make atonement for yourselves on the altar; it is the blood that makes atonement for one's life" (Leviticus 17:11).

When we jump to the New Testament, mere days before Christ's ultimate blood-shedding sacrifice, we see Him breaking bread and pouring a cup of red wine for His friends to share. Holding the cup, He says, "This is my blood of the covenant, which is poured out for many for the forgiveness of sins" (Matthew 26:28). I can just imagine the shock, surprise, and joy the disciples had during that gulp of Beaujolais.

Blood flows through generations and days, restoring life and hope. With lithe, graceful, almost airborne twisting, it moves through the pages of the Bible, history, and our lives. It transfuses and mediates grace in symbolic and real ways. Christ's blood comes to us a lot like the baby cardinal Cheri gave me. It comes in wisdom. It understands the pains and joys in our lives. It comes through words and images. It mediates grace and hope to our anemic souls.

The blood of goats and bulls and the ashes of a heifer sprinkled on those who are ceremonially unclean sanctify them so that they are outwardly clean. How much more, then, will the blood of Christ, who through the eternal Spirit offered himself unblemished to God, cleanse our consciences.

HEBREWS 9:13-14

Our Word—*Scriptures, Insights, & Suggestions*

1. If you're interested in tracing the red thread of God's love through the Old and New Testaments, take a few minutes to read these references to blood: Genesis 9:6; Exodus 12:13; 24:8; Leviticus 17:11; Psalm 72:14; Proverbs 6:17; Matthew 27:28; Romans 3:25; 5:9; 1 Corinthians 11:25; Ephesians 1:7, 2:13; Colossians 1:20; Hebrews 9:12,22; 1 Peter 1:19; 1 John 1:7; Revelation 1:5; 5:9; 7:14; 12:11. As you read, take notes, pray, and meditate. When you finish, write a poem, essay, journal entry, or song describing what this red thread means to you.

2. Is there something that symbolizes grace in your life? How does it show up during your days? How does it show up in God's Word?

3. Purchase a simple reminder of God's grace in your life: a plant, an image of a butterfly, a quilt, stained glass, a candle. Put it where you can be constantly reminded of the thread of God's love in your life.

*God was pleased to have his fullness dwell in him,
and through him to reconcile to himself all things
whether things on earth or things in heaven, by making
peace through his blood, shed on the cross.*

COLOSSIANS 1:19-20

11

Loving Your Neighbor

The Bible Moving in Next Door

*Where can I flee from your presence? If I go up to the
heavens, you are there…If I rise on the wings of the
dawn, if I settle on the far side of the sea, even there your
hand will guide me, your right hand will hold me fast.*

PSALM 139:7-10

Her Word—*Suzie's Residency*

I admit it. I'm not the best neighbor. In fact, if the people living in my block ran a sociability race, I'd definitely come in last place. During this energy-sucking season of mothering, I'm often depleted, having experienced little people overload. I know how insane it is to isolate myself, but after days on end of playing referee to my sons' wrestling matches; kissing dozens of nose to toes boo-boos (some real, others imagined) on my daughter's toddler frame; driving a crazy caravan of clamoring kids to bus stops, baseball games, soccer practices, and Kindermusic classes, my space for cordial conversation is usually drained, usurped, taken captive *Ransom of Red Chief* style.

I *want* to caravan and coddle and kiss my kids. I love and embrace being a mom. But mothering uses Herculean amounts of emotional energy, strength, and fortitude. Most days I *live* for my husband's return from work. I pass the parenting baton, along with our brimming brood, to him and set off for the sanctuary of Northside Park. It's the only moment during my day when I'm able to finish thoughts uninterrupted, take in sunsets or snowfalls in peaceful calm, breathe easily, pray, and let my muscles relax into the rhythm of my steps.

As I set out on my well-worn path, I freak out if I notice neighbors hanging out in their front yards looking ready and eager to "catch up" on news. Usually I pick up my pace, waving as I pass by. Then I wrestle with guilt, wondering why I have such a difficult time "loving my neighbors as myself." I'm sad that I don't connect with women and families who live near me. And so I ask God to open ways for me to get to know my neighbors without feeling even more wearied. At the same time I beg God to preserve and protect my times of solitude.

In spite of the prayers, connecting with neighbors was an exhausting expenditure for years. That all changed when Suzie moved in. Tall and lean, wearing a daily costume of blue jeans, a sweater, and sneakers, she's the embodiment of joy. A wife; a mother of two adolescent girls; and the owner of Cider, the smiling, auburn golden retriever, Suzie has an open, freckled face, hair the color of rust, and eyes of topaz blue. She's bottomlessly energetic, giving, convivial. When I'm trying to squeeze writing my magazine column into a hectic week, she often offers to play with my kids in the plastic pool in our shared backyards. When I'm feeling lonely she calls and offers leftovers and her company for lunch.

As my husband, Bryan, and I were getting ready to go to China to adopt Emily, Suzie planned a day in Chinatown for us. It was complete with our first ever dim sum brunch and a scavenger hunt (we had to find chopsticks, jade bracelets, a life-sized Buddha, etc.). When we finally brought Emily home, Suzie welcomed us with a king-sized sheet banner emblazoned with a greeting in Chinese characters hanging from our front porch.

The moment I knew Suzie and I were truly friends was the day she called around 5:30 on a weeknight to ask for a packet of taco seasoning. I'd embraced and enjoyed *all* the ways Suzie had poured her love and attention into my family and me over the years. Still, this simple request for something *I* could give, offer, do without and deplete my personal resources, deeply touched me. It may sound odd, but if I could've, I would have taken that request, like a rosebud, and pressed it between pages in a book.

Since the eve of the taco request I've purchased a special rug for my backdoor. (It's where Suz usually puts her boots or shoes when she stops over. Bry affectionately calls it our Suzie rug.) During the winter there are always footprints in the snow between Suzie's backdoor and mine. When I need an egg, some ginger, or a prayer, she's the first friend I call.

Lately—and surprisingly—I've even invited Suzie to share the sacred sanctum of my daily walk. Something about walking alongside her, sharing the journey of life, is comforting. I also find it companionable when I look out my kitchen window and see lights on in her house. We tease each other about being "peeping toms." When our husbands are out of town or on particularly lonely Sunday afternoons, it's nice to see the soft, yellow glow in each other's windows. It reminds us that we're not alone.

> *When someone says to us in the midst of a crisis,*
> *"I do not know what to do, but I want you to realize*
> *that I am with you, that I will not leave you alone,"*
> *we have a friend through whom we can find*
> *consolation and comfort.*[1]
>
> HENRI NOUWEN

God's Word—*Our Neighbor*

> *The Word became flesh and blood,*
> *and moved into the neighborhood.*
>
> JOHN 1:14 MSG

Sometimes I wonder if our Bibles collect dust because we consider them like nosy neighbors wanting to meddle in our lives, offer unsolicited advice, and ask for favors we're not ready to satisfy. Perhaps we're afraid to crack open the pages because we think reading Scripture might captivate us, expect something of us, change us, and make demands on our already depleted selves. I've found that sometimes it's easier to conserve energy and the status quo of life. The dichotomy is that interacting and being open to people and words ultimately enriches us.

In New Testament times Jesus was the Word made flesh who moved around Galilee, Samaria, and Judea. He made crazy claims, turned tables on religious tradition, infected the sinew of people's lives. Some set down fishing nets, climbed trees, made sojourns, came back to wells to be near Jesus. Others washed their hands of His claims, turned their backs, and walked away. Which example will we follow?

Though we're not able to physically get next to the incarnate Christ, His words live as near to us as our next-door neighbors. In America, they sit in almost every bookstore, every library, on the shelves and in hope chests of many households. We can choose to give an imperious wave and walk by, or we can get to know the words and meanings and truths by inviting them in the way I let Suzie in.

At first I wasn't sure I had the energy to keep up with Suzie's joviality, adventure planning, and close proximity. But now that

I've let her in on my walks and into my kitchen, I'm glad Suzie moved into the neighborhood!

God's Word is trustworthy and right. If we open ourselves to its wisdom, it will not drain, deplete, and diminish us. I love the verse in Isaiah that notes, "A bruised reed he will not break" (42:3). God is not waiting to pounce, desiring to get us in His clutches until we are broken and bruised and conformed to His image. He loves us. He patiently whispers words of grace into our ready, open, needy places.

God's words will not pound themselves into our heads. They might shock, surprise, or catch us off guard, but they'll also comfort, encourage, and support. And just like Suzie's taco seasoning request, when and if God's Word demands something from us, we'll be ready. And God will equip us for whatever task He puts before us. And more often than not the request will be exactly what we've been yearning for or needing to give: a little more patience, money, devotion, attention, mercy, time, surrender, love.

And then, amazingly, as we continue to invite God's words into our lives we'll receive the comfort and companionship of a God whose name is Immanuel, "God with us!" We'll know that Divinity abides in our neighborhoods. Though Christ is not physically walking our streets, He makes Himself near, accessible, and audible through the written Word. Anytime we feel alone, or confused, or discouraged; anytime we need a promise of light and life, we can find it in the pages of the Bible.

Psalm 119:130 reads, "The unfolding of your words gives light." After I read that psalm last night I turned off my bedside lamp and looked out my window. Every window in Suzie's home was brimming with amber luminescence. In that moment I couldn't help but hope that as we unfold God's Word we will sense the bright, warm, next-door nearness of The Word spilling brightly into our neighborhoods.

*The God-with-us is a close God, a God whom we call our
refuge, our stronghold, our wisdom, and even,
more intimately, our helper, our shepherd, our love.
We will never really know God as a compassionate
God if we do not understand with our hearts and minds
that He lives among us.*

Our Word—*Scriptures, Insights, & Suggestions*

1. What is your relationship with your neighbors? If you feel isolated from some of them, consider hosting a simple brunch or coffee to get to know one another. Or simply ask your neighbor if you can borrow a cup of sugar.

2. Do you ever see the Bible as an annoying, nosy neighbor who wants to drain energy out of your life? Instead, picture the God who loves you next door. He wants to add joy and help and companionship to your life!

3. Read Psalm 119:129-136 and paraphrase it in your journal as a prayer of your heart.

Love your neighbor as yourself.

Matthew 19:19

12

A True Page-Turner

Wisdom, Mercy, and Incredible Stories

I brought home my first Bible in February 1982, the month I awakened to the reality of Christ as the Living Word of God. I'd always seen the Bible as a dry, boring collection of archaic rules. Imagine my surprise when I discovered it was a life-changing book filled with wisdom, grace, and incredible stories. Talk about a page-turner![1]

LIZ CURTIS HIGGS

Her Word—*Cheri's Stories*

Cheri is an excellent storyteller. She's the most observant, intuitive friend I have. An introvert at heart, she's usually not the first woman to chime in during gatherings with girlfriends. But when Cheri starts talking, all ears in the room bend toward her like sunflowers searching for rays. I'm reminded of the old E.F. Hutton commercial, "When E.F. Hutton talks…people listen!"

Cheri has an uncanny way of remembering little details, such as the precise moment a friend took a sip of her green tea, the slant of light during a conversation, the exact phrasing of a sentence. And she has an artful way of adding experiences together in an equation that inevitably yields wisdom, mercy, and goose bumps. These skills make her an exceptional writer and priceless friend.

When I think of Cher, the last line of E.B. White's *Charlotte's Web* often floats to the surface of my mind. In this passage, Wilbur (the pig) fondly remembers Charlotte (the spider and heroine), who has written him out of death's harm on numerous occasions by stitching words into her web. "She was in a class by herself. It is not often that someone comes along who is a true friend and a good writer. Charlotte was both," Wilbur states.

Cheri is both too. Just the other day I was putting away canned goods, apples, and milk while we talked on the phone. An hour into the conversation, I found myself sitting at the kitchen table. From my chair I noticed the carton of 2% milk covered in thousands of sweaty beads warming on my counter. That's when I realized Cheri had entangled me in her web of words again.

I can't remember the story exactly, but I think it began with enthusiasm about a recent church sermon and then spun into a discourse on "Thin Places." Cheri animatedly explained that a "Thin Place" is where the veil between this world and heaven is particularly skinny. "Naked, raw, almost tangible truths abide in Thin Places," she said, "along with the comfort and fortitude to help us deal."

I was struck by the thought that Cheri's stories are Thin Places to me. They always reveal gracious realities that connect my daily life to the divine.

Whether I'm reading one of Cher's articles, visiting her in Minnesota, helping proof her latest book, or cowriting a manuscript with her (such as our recent *Play with Me: Two Friends on a Spiritual Journey with Kids*), I'm always delighted by Cheri's uncanny way of showing the salt and pepper relationship between the holy and the human. It doesn't matter if Cheri's telling the story of a recent romp at the park with her kids, her latest garage sale conquest, or a tender moment with her husband, Rich, she uses vivid sensory descriptors, narrative twists, tension builders, and even comic relief. She knows just when to pause, just how much detail to include, just the way to reveal the moral of the stories:

> *The more I let go, the more I become...There is no such thing
> as a perfect friend. But there are friends who are perfect for
> us...If we think we have it all figured out, and that we know
> God's mind on all things, then we deceive ourselves. The less
> we know, the more we are free to know...On the other hand,
> I thank God that he didn't leave us without* any *direction.
> We have the Bible, and the Holy Spirit, and the testimony of
> people who have gone before us.*

Anytime I listen to Cher, I risk spoiled milk. It's worth it though.
When I'm enraptured in her stories, I inevitably end up in the Thin
Place where wisdom and mercy are fully tangible.

God's Word—*A Good Read*

> *God is a great storyteller,
> and the Bible is the greatest of all storybooks.*[2]
>
> MADELEINE L'ENGLE

Many think the Bible is filled with dos and don'ts and as dry
as a bunch of brittle bones. Granted, if you limit your reading to
Leviticus, that may be correct. The broader reality, though, is that
the Bible is as alive and as exhilarating as listening to Cheri or
reading the latest Jodi Picoult novel! Who would've thought the
Bible is filled with the historical intrigue of a docudrama, the sus-
pense of a good thriller, the sexual tension of a romance novel, and
the excellent writing of a piece of literary fiction?

Sometimes we read God's Word expecting to get banged over the
head with laws and commands. But if we open the pages expecting
to find thrilling, truth-telling, *NY Times* bestselling stories, poetry,
prose, proverbs, and life-changing morals, we'll end up in a Thin
Place where wisdom and mercy live.

Many are familiar with the stories of *The Creation, Adam and Eve, Cain and Abel, Noah's ark, Samson and Delilah,* and *The Exodus.* There are other "less known yet equally page-turning stories" distinctly about women that are worth checking out (or rereading): *Hannah's struggle with infertility* (1 Samuel 1), *the woman of Endor and her compassion on Saul* (1 Samuel 28:3-25), *Queen Esther's foiling of Haman's Hitler-like plot against the Jews* (Esther 3–4 and 7–9), *Gomer's true love* (Hosea 1–3), and my personal favorite, *the woman who touched the hem of Jesus' garment* (Mark 5:25-34).

These tales, in and of themselves, are worth our time. They entertain, give us a sense of God's work through history, make us feel companioned. They also bring us to a Thin Place, a place closer to heaven...A place where we discover the grandest, most spellbinding morals imaginable: *The underdogs win* (Matthew 19:30), *love conquers death* (John 13:1; 1 Corinthians 15:21), *power arrives on the shoulders of weakness* (2 Corinthians 12:9), *by letting go desires are granted* (Matthew 16:25), and *God's wisdom may appear foolish* (1 Corinthians 1:18). They bring us to a place where God's wisdom and mercy touch us in heart-changing ways.

So many times we pick up the Bible for a quick fix, to complete an obligatory Bible study, or to assuage a self-imposed spiritual guilt trip. Perhaps we would enjoy God's Word more if we saw it as a delectable page-turner, a "life-changing book filled with wisdom, mercy, and incredible stories."

Together let's look for life and love, drama and delight, excitement and enlightenment in the parchment pages. And perhaps we'll be as inclined to pick up our Bibles as I am to call Cher with the hope of hearing a great story with spiritual significance.

Our Word—*Scriptures, Insights, & Suggestions*

1. Do you perceive the Bible as being filled with intrigue, drama, romance, and truth? Or do you think of it as a dull, dusty tome? Why?

2. Purchase or check out from the library the Bible on CD. Or find an online version to download. I recently discovered online audio Bibles with sound effects, music, and more. Yesterday I even found a Mandarin version! Listen to a few chapters the way you used to listen to bedtime stories as a child or the way you listen to the good stories of a friend. Describe your experience.

3. The next time you pick up your Bible, consider your motivations. Why are you prompted to read? What are you expecting from the book? Why?

> *And because I read the Bible as a storybook,*
> *not a moral tract (which it is not), I read it with pleasure*
> *(surely God's Word should be pleasing to us!),*
> *and I read it for fun. I read it as play, not work,*
> *and surely that is how it ought to be read.*
> *Jesus had a marvelous sense of fun, of play.*[3]
>
> MADELEINE L'ENGLE

$$\boxed{13}$$

I Give You My Word

God's Word Holds Promises

> *Promises are made with words...*
> *[And] part of myself that goes with every promise is*
> *given to you through my words.*[1]
>
> MICHAEL CARD

Her Word—*Heather's Promising Prayers*

Whenever I need prayer, Heather ("the Magnet") is one of the faith-filled women I call. She has a way of seeing me (and my problems) and praying with words infused with poignant, perfectly selected, promising verses from the Bible. When "the Magnet" prays for me I'm surprised by how much of herself she pours into the prayer. She almost becomes a two-way mirror reflecting me to myself, and then refracting the powerful image of God, as seen through His Word, into my difficulties.

Recently she prayed that I would meet a writing deadline, that my words would touch the hearts of women, and that at the end of my arduous work times I would have energy to avail myself to my children. Artfully and wisely, she punctuated each intercession with a paraphrase of one of God's promises to make the truth come alive in my situation.

1. That I would meet my deadline: "Be strong and coura-
geous, and do the work. Do not be afraid or discouraged
by the size of the task, for the Lord God is with you.
He will see to it that all the work is finished correctly"
(1 Chronicles 28:20). As my inspirational friend prayed, I
felt a swelling of strength and courage rising up in my chest.
My soul was stilled as I found a gracing perspective envi-
sioning *God* seeing to it that my work would get finished.

2. That my words would touch the hearts of women: "May
the favor of the Lord your God rest upon you; establish
the work of your hands for you—yes, establish the work
of your hands" (Psalm 90:17). What a sense of shared sisterhood I felt with Heather as she prayed for the work of
my hands. What a sense of peace I also felt realizing that
it was not *my* job to establish the work of my hands. I just
had to do the work. *God* Almighty would establish, use,
and send it forth.

3. That I would have energy to avail myself to my children:
"Hannah said, "I asked the LORD to give me this child,
and he has given me my request. Now I am giving him to
the LORD, and he will belong to the LORD his whole life"
(1 Samuel 1:27-28 NLT). The words reminded me of Hannah's struggle with infertility and the way God answered
her prayer. They also reminded me of unique ways God
answered my prayer by giving me two biological sons and
one adopted daughter. It refreshed me to imagine Samuel
and each of my brimming brood as belonging to the Lord.
I was reminded that He would help raise, sustain, love,
and mother His babes.

Almost two decades ago, when I was struggling with singleness, Heather prayed for me then too. I'd cry and moan about stag
Valentine's Days and other holidays. I'd worry about my ticking
child-bearing clock. She'd pray, "Lord, remind Sally that You are
her husband 'your Maker is your husband—the LORD Almighty

is his name. The Holy One of Israel is your Redeemer' (Isaiah 54:5) The God of all the earth loves you." Heather continued, "And, Lord, deeply instill the truth that You want to give Sally the desires of her heart: 'Delight yourself in the LORD and he will give you the desires of your heart'" (Psalm 37:4).

In those days, when Heather finished praying, I'd inevitably and often complain that God seemed to be sleeping on the job, and I was tired of waiting. Heather would take a deep breath and start praying again.

I can just hear her inhaling, revving up again, "Father, be with Sally. We believe that Your ways are higher than our ways [Isaiah 55:8] and that You make all things beautiful in Your time" [Ecclesiastes 3:11]. I remember how I felt each time "the Mag" finished praying for me. A sense of peace and new perspective washed over me like a sunny summer shower. Knowing that Heather put her words and herself into God's promises helped me believe that God would do the same.

> *The Lord is not slow in keeping his promise,*
> *as some understand slowness.*
>
> 1 PETER 3:9

God's Word—*God's Vows*

> *Our God is the great maker of promises.*
> *His Word, the Bible is quite simply a collection of the*
> *promises He has made to us.*[2]
>
> MICHAEL CARD

We're all in need of God's redemptive, healing, buoying

promises. And, thank goodness, His Word is full of them. Years ago I wrote capital P's in the margin of my Bible each time I discovered a divine promise. I quickly curtailed that practice when plentiful P's began dotting my NIV's pages like a bad case of chicken pox.

As an homage to Heather, and an intercession, will you pray the following prayer with me?

> *Promising Father,*
>
> *We love You and thank You for being a God of Promises. We know for every predicament or joy facing this circle of girl-friends, You offer hope and the fulfillment of Your promises.*
>
> *For those of us longing for physical healing, You promise You are the Lord who heals. For those of us yearning that the rifts in relationships be restored, You set the lonely [the singles] in families. For those rejoicing at a gift, success, or victory, You will bless them in their harvest and in all the work of their hands, and their joy will be complete. For those who have said goodbye to or recently buried a friend or family member, You say, "[My] loved ones are precious to [me]; it grieves [me] when they die. [I] will swallow up death forever. [I] will wipe away the tears from all faces." For those of us longing for a child, You promise "[I] settle the barren woman in her home as a happy mother of children." And for those of us living under the darkness of depression, You assure us that Your joy is our strength.*
>
> *As we pray these promises and search for more in Your holy Scriptures, we realize that Your Son is the ultimate promise. One of His names is "the Promise." We believe that in Him all Your oaths, vows, words, and hopes come true. Thank You, God! Amen.*

If you'd like to read more on these promises, check out Exodus 15:26; Psalm 68:6; Deuteronomy 16:15; Psalm 1116:15 NLT; Isaiah 25:8 NIV; Psalm 113:9; and Nehemiah 8:10.

*In the fullness of time what God had desired to do
through the ages happened: He gave all of Himself to us
through Jesus Christ, the Word of God, spoken
at an incalculable price.*[3]

MICHAEL CARD

Our Word—*Scriptures, Insights, & Suggestions*

1. Is there a particular promise from the Bible you want to claim as yours right now? Write it on a 3 x 5 card and place it where you'll see it throughout your day. Bask in the refreshment of the promise.

2. If you or a friend need prayer, get together for coffee and pray Scripture into each other's broken, needy, dry, or barren places.

3. Write a "P" in the margin of your Bible each time you encounter one of God's promises. If you choose to do this, notice the chicken pox effect.

*Let us hold unswervingly to the hope we profess,
for he who promised is faithful.*

HEBREWS 10:23

14

Glow Sticks

The Bible as Illuminator

The LORD is my shepherd, I shall not want.
He makes me lie down in green pastures,
he leads me beside quiet waters, he restores my soul.

PSALM 23:1-3

Her Word—*Heather's Light Dance*

I have a summer birthday. June 23, to be exact. I rejoice in that. Strawberries, lightning bugs, swimming, running barefoot in the grass, camping under a tent of stars are part of the playful season during which I was born.

One summer, the day before my birthday, Heather ("the Magnet") came for a spontaneous, unexpected visit. She didn't realize my birthday was approaching. She never knows when it's my birthday because it's not in her nature to remember dates. I don't take it personally, and I enjoy her belated birthday cards that often come as autumn leaves fall or even when it's snowing. The Magnet has a million special, touching, meaningful ways of celebrating me even when it's not my birthday, and I love her for that.

When "the Mag" called on June 22, to say she'd be traveling through Illinois with her little girl and little boy, I couldn't wait to fill up our plastic pool, make water balloons, and collect fixings for s'mores.

"Don't tell her tomorrow's my birthday," I warned Bryan, not wanting the Magnet to feel bad.

By the time the Mag and her miniature but boisterous crew arrived they were too tired for a campfire. We exchanged bear hugs, and I showed them to their beds. As I fell asleep, I imagined the next day as a celebration of summer fun. I pictured Heather and me sipping tall glasses of homemade lemonade, dipping our feet into the Elmo pool and having a "Hen Party" while our rambunctious little buddies ran through the sprinkler, spit watermelon seeds, and played together in obedient harmony.

The next morning I was in the kitchen flipping pancakes and slicing strawberries when I heard Heather shuffle toward me.

She slumped down in a chair at the kitchen table, hardly able to hold up her head. She barely eked out, "Sal...I'm...not...feeling too...good." She placed her head in her hands and rubbed her forehead. I knew instantly something was terribly wrong with my normally zany girlfriend.

"What's goin' on?" I asked, turning off the burner and walking toward her. The nearer I got, the greener her skin looked.

As if tapping out Morse code from behind enemy lines, she answered, "I didn't...sleep...all night. My throat is so...swollen...I can hardly swallow. I think I'm running a...fever."

I could tell Heather felt flatter than the pancakes I was frying. She definitely needed to see a doctor. As quiet as snow and as swift as sound I gathered Heather's purse and shoes. I wrote out directions to the nearest urgent care facility and helped her to her car. As I watched her drive away, I wished I could be driving my friend to the doc, but with Bryan at work and five sleeping kids upstairs, someone needed to "woman" the fort...in spite of her birthday.

An hour or so later the kids were using their last few bites of pancakes to soak up syrup when an exhausted, fever-ravaged Heather returned with a diagnosis and an antibiotic. "It's strep throat," she said gingerly, flinging her purse and keys onto my couch and collapsing.

"I'm soooooo sorry!" I said as I brought water to help Heather down her pills and an extra blanket for the bed where she'd convalesce all day. She tried to sleep; I tried to play with the kids. I could feel a bad attitude incubating in me. It was going to be a long, sweaty summer day for Heather *and* me.

My hopes for "a celebration of summer fun" disintegrated five minutes after breakfast. The five kids ran away from the table in five different directions. The chaos continued with requests for five different snacks every five minutes. I finally corralled them, and we headed to the park. I almost plummeted over the mothering edge when the tiniest in the troupe needed to use the bathroom five blocks away from the park that seemed to take five hours to reach.

I tried to shift my expectations and enter into the kids' play, looking for something to be thankful for. But it didn't help. The day dragged on and on. It felt like *five*ver until Bryan would be home to help herd the quintet.

When he finally arrived, I experienced a mirage. I saw Bryan wearing a red cape, tights, and a huge "S" on a muscle-bound chest. He flexed one rippling bicep in order to elevate a pizza above his head. *Did he really bring home pizza?* The aroma of cheese and sausage answered affirmatively and brought me back to reality. I rushed to hug and kiss my hubby and grab a slice.

The Magnet emerged from her hellish hole halfway through dinner. We sat side by side on my love seat, eating pizza and looking like war-torn combatants. The food and companionship of adults energized both of us enough to crack smiles at one another. Somehow I rallied enough to grab a paper sack and ask everyone to gather on the front porch.

The sun had just pulled a pink ribbon across the sky and then rested behind the hill by our pond. Heather, wrapped in a blanket and buoyed by Amoxicillin, sat on the front steps. The kids ran around the front yard, in paths as circuitous as the fireflies.

"Guess what's in here?" I asked holding up the sack.

The children lined up. "Candy, a puppy, fireworks…a monster," they shouted with glee and anticipation.

I opened the bag to reveal dozens of twisted, illuminated glow sticks. With my day's first breath of pure joy, I handed them out. The kids adorned themselves with belts, earrings, necklaces, head-dresses, and anklets of glowing summer frivolity. Bryan grabbed a boom box and blasted Huey Lewis' *The Power of Love.* In sync with the sax and to the beat of the drums, the children twirled and twisted, jived and jumped.

I don't know how it happened, but two glow sticks got left in the bag. Heather grabbed one for herself and handed the other one to me. Before we knew it we were dancing in the grass, swirling shimmering sticks raised to the sky. Who would've thought that light could come out of such darkness?

> *You, O LORD, keep my lamp burning;*
> *my God turns my darkness into light.*
>
> PSALM 18:28

God's Word—*Our Light on the Path*

> *Your word is a lamp to my feet and a light for my path.*
>
> PSALM 119:105

During some of the darkest times in my life, God's Word has shed illuminating light, hope, and radiance on my path. When I was suffering with the worst of my chronic, excruciating back pain, Exodus 15:26 brought me God's comfort: "I am the LORD, who heals you." I returned to these words time and again, not expecting God to give me a cure for my degenerated disc (though He could certainly do that if He chose). I read the words over and over again to remind me that God, by His nature, is a healing Lord. He cares, offers comfort, and gives hope. One day He'll give me complete healing—mind, body, and soul.

Even as I read "I am the LORD, who heals you" this morning, I notice my achy back. It's a bummer to be a passionate, wild woman who has to struggle to bend over and suffers severe pain if she stands for too long. But I'm truly comforted because I believe God is doing a healing work, even now, through my pain. He's making me sensitive to others who live with pain or disability. He's allowing me the gift to slow down because of my weakness so I can rest my weary body in loving arms.

When I was newly married, I also experienced a time of hideous darkness in my life. This darkness came in the form of a rift between my dad and me. Because of the growing pains of my new union with Bryan, bonds with my father stretched to a breaking point. Some of these bonds were enmeshed, codependent, and unhealthy. They needed to be relinquished, redeemed, reformed. And, by God's grace, new, healthy bonds are daily being established.

Still, though it was necessary, the almost two-year period of time during which I was disconnected from my father was very painful. Friends helped, a counselor helped, prayer helped. And the light of Scripture on my darkened road helped too. At each turn along the journey, God had new words of hope, and help, and healing.

One of the bright verses was Psalm 16:5-6: "LORD, you have assigned me my portion and my cup; you have made my lot secure. The boundary lines have fallen for me in pleasant places; surely I have a delightful inheritance." Being disconnected from my dad was scary. I felt lonely and desired his companionship, approval, and hugs. These verses in Psalms made it clear God was with me and that the boundaries I was establishing during my early days of marriage would land in pleasant places. And there was God's promise of a delightful inheritance in my life. Even today my path is illuminated by that passage as I live out a relationship of loving, growing with, and forgiving my father.

I don't think it was a haphazard coincidence that Christ quoted Scripture during His crucifixion. It makes me sad beyond belief to imagine Jesus, who is one with God, who *is* God, feeling forsaken by God. I know Christ was in excruciating pain. I know He was struggling for each breath, pulling Himself up by nail-shattered wrists for each inhalation. I know He was sweating blood and saying goodbye to friends and His mother. I know He was in His life's darkest moment. Yet I wonder if crying out to God with David's prophetic words of Psalm 22 shed light on His darkened path. I believe Christ used the words—an expression of His dying heart—to honor and be real with His Father. As He died on the cross, almost every detail of the crucifixion was soaked in prophecy: His thirst, His divided garments, His unbroken legs...I've often thought about Christ's last words, *"Eloi, Eloi, lama sabachthani?"* which means "My God, my God, why have you forsaken me?" I also imagine that though He did not have the physical strength to speak the rest of Psalm 22, perhaps He continued mentally through the text:

> I am a worm and not a man, scorned by men and despised by the people. All who see me mock me; they hurl insults, shaking their heads...I am poured out like water, and all my bones are out of joint. My heart has turned to wax; it has melted away within me. My strength is dried up...my tongue sticks to the roof of my mouth; you lay me in the dust of death. Dogs have surrounded me; a band of evil men has encircled me, they have pierced my hands and my feet (Psalm 22:6-7,14-16).

And perhaps right before Jesus died He began quoting the next psalm: "The LORD is my shepherd, I shall not want..." Perhaps the words brought light to His path, affirming His fulfillment of Old Testament prophecy, completing His mission, connecting Him with God and the divine purpose in a most intimate way. I'm comforted to think my Savior's Passion was lightened by David's words.

I know that disappointing time of my birthday, my trials with back pain, and the trials with my parents are nothing compared to the crucifixion. I'm thankful, nevertheless, for God's wisdom and comfort that come during life's darkest moments...just like glow sticks lighting up a summer's night.

> *And then the sun rose and Jesus was alive and terror fled*
> *and the Resurrection was an inner brightness...*
> *And that light, inner and outer began its journey around*
> *the earth, the solar systems, the furthest galaxies, light*
> *that is not power, but is wholly love.*[1]
>
> MADELEINE L'ENGLE

Our Word—*Scriptures, Insights, & Suggestions*

1. Can you remember a dark season in your life? Did the Bible illuminate your way during that time? Why or why not?

2. If you're facing a time of darkness, read Psalm 22 and Psalm 23. Memorize passages that touch your heart from these chapters. Meditate on these during transitional or particularly difficult moments in your days.

3. Paint a picture, write a poem, or journal about the way God brings light into your darkness through Scripture.

> *I will love the light for it shows me the way. Yet I will*
> *endure the darkness for it shows me the stars.*
>
> OG MANDINO

15

Spices, Perfumes, Stories

The Bible Caring for Our Needs

*Carry each other's burdens, and in this way
you will fulfill the law of Christ.*

GALATIANS 6:2

Pray for each other so that you may be healed.

JAMES 5:16

Her Word—*Chanhassen Mirrors*

I went to a book signing in my friend and coauthor's hometown of Chanhassen, Minnesota. Women from adjoining communities were gathering at C.J.'s Coffee and Wine Bar at Market Street Station to hear Cheri and me read snippets from our latest book, *Play with Me: Two Friends on a Spiritual Journey with Kids.*

Cheri and I were both exhausted. I was drained from the drive up to Minnesota and, really, the entire last year of my life adjusting to my newly adopted daughter. Cheri was depleted from the usual drains of motherhood and an unexpected job change for her husband that left her family in a financial crunch. We were looking forward to the evening though, and entered the artsy, cozy, dimly lit, friendly atmosphere of C.J.'s hoping for God's sustenance and help.

Cher and I sat on tall stools sharing a microphone and a few stories about the torturous and terrific nature of motherhood. I told about my recent trip to China to adopt my daughter. Cheri caused women of all ages (including me) to snort with laughter and understanding as she read her famous "recipe" for burnt toast.

> *Ingredients/Utensils:* One piece of whole-wheat bread, three small children, a toaster, knife, and one working smoke detector.
>
> *Directions:* Help daughter finish her "impossible, stupid, I-hate-homework" math while strapping screaming, kicking toddler in highchair and explaining to preschool son why a tank top during a blizzard might be a fashion faux pas. Begin preparing school lunches, a literal assembly line of PB & J sandwiches while trying to recall the definition of "hypotenuse" and reiterating the importance of brushing one's teeth to son who is still begging to wear the tank top.
>
> Sing "C is for cookie and cookie starts with C" in an attempt to calm still screaming toddler...Explain to daughter that math is not your forte, which is why hypotenuse sounds like a thyroid medication while spoon-feeding toddler and shushing tank-top clad son who has taken over singing "Cookie, cookie" in a heavy-metal rock star style. Piercing sound of smoke detector shocks everyone into a fit of tears. Consider toast done, well done...just the way you like it.

During a "Mothering Confessions" portion of the evening, I exposed my son's fearsome revelation that "Mrs. Gloz, Matthew's mom, has a cleaner bathroom than ours!" Cheri unloaded "The Tale of a Toddler, a White Couch, and a Permanent Black Sharpie Marker."

Along with exposing some of our parenting foibles and failures, we talked about times of sparkling, unexpected joy when our children helped us see the divine in the daily. Times when they helped us recognize the wind as God's breath and feel breathed on by His Spirit. Times when they helped us see trees and toads, sunsets and skyscrapers for the first time...*again*. Times when they reminded us what it's like to be small, curious, open-minded, imaginative, and exploratory. Times when they taught us why Jesus said, "Unless you change and become like little children, you will never enter the kingdom of heaven" (Matthew 18:3).

Between story sets, a local musician—Carol Zimmerman— shared her mothering insights via a warm alto voice and arpeggiated guitar chords. After her last cadence faded, Cher and I returned to entertain a few audience questions. It didn't surprise us one bit when questions of mothering and writing turned to questions about our friendship.

> *Where and when did you meet?*
>
> *How do you maintain and cultivate a friendship when you live 400 miles away from each other?*
>
> *What's the secret to your close-knit friendship?*

As always, we did our best to explain that God has been the Maker and Sustainer of our relationship. He's the one who unexpectedly paired us—two women as opposite as the sun and moon—as suite mates at Wheaton College more than two decades ago. He's the one who gives us creative ways to stay connected: reading books, writing books, celebrating life's passages, sharing stories, praying for one another.

While we were mentioning these things, two women sitting at a round table near the stage wildly wagged their heads in agreement. One of them was a beautiful blond wearing stylish square glasses and denim. In "Ooooo, Oooooo, Mr. Kotter, Mr. Kotter!" fashion, she raised her hand and added to our commentary. "Friendship is what women *need*," she emphatically stated. "Yes, some of us are called to marriage and family. But *all* of us need friends—deep, gritty, real, daily friends to call and pray with and share in life's journey."

Our beautiful blond sister continued her soapbox plea for deeper connections woman-to-woman. She explained that we need to "care for one another, be there for each other." Cheri and I felt we should turn the microphone over to our passionate new girlfriend. She was inspiring! We felt as if we were looking at a reflection of ourselves in this woman and her friend. At the same time, we were surprised, soaking up her words that slaked us after having spilled ourselves out for others. We thanked both women for being there and buoying and blessing us and the entire gathering.

At the end of the evening, as we cleaned up our book table and helped Carol stack her speakers by the door, we noticed the boisterous blond and her friend were still savoring last sips of coffee. After Cheri and I signed our last book, the women approached with hugs and the offer to pray for us.

In the corner by the front door, as women donned jackets to meet Minnesota's cold, dark night, the two wild, wagging women prayed for Cheri and me. They poured their words to God, asking for blessings on our husbands, protection for our children, multiplication of the fruit from our writing and speaking. Cheri held out her hand to receive God's blessing. I held out mine too. The blond woman's friend placed her hand underneath mine—supporting, caring for, and sustaining me. We didn't expect this. We will never forget it. A beautiful time of women gathering together, ministering to one another in story and word and prayer, caring for one another.

God's Word—*Two Marys and More*

Many women were there, watching from a distance. They had followed Jesus from Galilee to care for his needs. Among them were Mary Magdalene, Mary the mother of James and Joses, and the mother of Zebedee's sons.

MATTHEW 27:55-56

The day after our Chanhassen gig, I sat by a sunny window of a bagel shop. I sipped hazelnut coffee and munched a pumpkin bagel while reading some of my favorite passages in the Gospels. I love turning to them after rich experiences with friends. The words and situations are thick with feelings of community, friendship, Jesus as best friend, beloved, missed, life of the party.

First I read about the Last Supper. Next was the death of Jesus, His burial, and the intoxicating passages where He rises from the dead and appears—first to Mary Magdalene (a woman from whom He earlier cast out seven demons). I embrace this story! I love that Jesus revealed Himself to a woman first—and especially a woman with a past. I love that Mary, unchecked, ran toward the risen Christ to smother Him with hugs and kisses. I love that Jesus asked her not to hold on to Him, but, instead, go tell His 12 forlorn friends He was alive! I imagine Mary's arms pumping and can practically hear her feet tearing up a dusty path, smell her sweat, feel her heart pounding along the way.

I also read the warm, unfathomable passages where Jesus hooked up with His brokenhearted, mournful friends on the road to Emmaus, on a beach where they were fishing, and at a bonfire where He fried up the catch of the day. I could almost smell the smoke, taste the flaky, flavorful fish, and experience the joy of reuniting. I flipped from Matthew to Mark, John to Luke, and relished the scenes, the sights, and the dialogs.

I also drew upon my recent connections with Cheri and the women at C.J.'s. I'd just had dinner with Cheri and another sweet friend and, in a small way, I could imagine the intimacy, laughter, and poignancy of the Last Supper. Since I had just hugged my friend goodbye, I could, in a small way, imagine what the disciples felt when they said goodbye to their best friend and teacher—the best fisherman they'd ever met. I'd experienced the heart-pounding joy of sharing the living Christ with a group of women who wanted to find Him in the daily drudgery of their lives. In a small way I could imagine the intensity of Mary Magdalene's dash to tell the 12 she'd met Jesus at the tomb.

With a last bite of bagel on my plate, I noticed a verse I didn't remember from previous readings: Matthew 27:55. It notes that "many women were there [at the cross], watching from a distance." It also says that these women, including Mary Magdalene, Mary the mother of James and Joses, and the mother of Zebedee's sons, followed Jesus to the cross all the way from Galilee. Most importantly...and beguilingly...the verse mentions that the women had made the journey *to care for Christ's needs.*

I read the verse over and over, letting it soak me like a warm summer rain. I imagined the trek from Galilee to Golgotha. Jesus led the sorrowful way. The women followed at a respectable distance. They were laden with perfumes, spices, and *stories.* They knew where they were going, so in memoriam, they more than likely retold tales of Christ as a child, Christ as an adolescent, Christ as the man who had become their Friend-Redeemer. Their stories salved each other in the same way their spices and perfumes would salve the body of Christ.

Jesus cared for these women. These women cared for Him. Cheri and I had cared for women. Women, in an unexpected turn, had cared for us. Now I sat at a twenty-first-century bagel shop reading my Bible and realizing that just like the many women who cared for Christ, and just like the women who cared for Cheri and me, the biblical stories were, in fact, caring for me: soothing like rare perfumes and spices.

> *[Women of the Bible] are real women who struggled with tragedy...who risked their lives and their reputations for the sake of others, whose compassion and wisdom often saved the day...Their stories reveal so much about God's love, his relentless jealousy, and his creative ability to bring good out of the most desperate of circumstances.*[1]
>
> ANN SPANGLER AND JEAN E. SYSWERDA

Our Word—*Scriptures, Insights, & Suggestions*

1. What is your favorite Bible story? Read it again and meditate on how it relates to your own stories.

2. Write a midrash, montage, paraphrase, or poem about your favorite Bible story. Interweave sounds, sights, smells, tastes, touches, and feelings from your life to vivify the biblical one. Share your writings with a friend.

3. Do you feel cared for when you read God's Word? Why or why not? Sing a song, write a poem, or create a piece of art to express your feelings about this.

For the past three years [Mary Magdalene] had followed the rabbi across Galilee and Judea, providing for him out of her own small purse. She had loved his hearty laughter and the smile that flashed across his face whenever he saw her. Wherever they went, she felt privileged to tell her story, grateful to be among his growing band of follwers.[2]

Ann Spangler and Jean E. Syswerda

Filling in the Blanks

Scripture Knows Our Stories

> *When you're a child, your friends are how you spend your*
> *time. When you're a teen, they help define you,*
> *dispel your only-ness. When you're grown up,*
> *they bring you news of the finiteness of things;*
> *they bring you flowers. They bring you back to your own*
> *memories by unveiling some of theirs.*[1]

BETH KEPHART

Her Word—*Memory Lane with Margie*

During my freshman year at Wheaton College I took many midnight walks to Dunkin Donuts on the edge of town. The walks traversed over a mile of tree-lined streets dotted with houses that seemed to smile beneath vine veils. The walks were invigorating, healthy. With donuts at the exercise's finish line, I gained the ubiquitous "Freshman Fifteen."

Donut runs continued during my sophomore year. And on one fall evening as crisp as a Granny Smith, I included Margie, an ebullient freshman, on one of my pilgrimages to glazed ecstasy and coffee. Earlier in the week I'd heard Margie confidently telling her roommate of plans to be the first female president of the United States. In that moment I knew we were destined to be friends.

As Margie and I walked along Main Street accompanied by the din of cricket arpeggios and the lingering aroma of sunset among trees, we talked. Remembering how I missed the propinquity of childhood friends, I said, "I know how it feels to be new around this place, Margie. It's kind of tough asking someone who hardly knows you for a seat at their lunch table, a shoulder to cry on, or even a tampon when you've run out."

Margie agreed. Over the next few blocks she told me about the ritual way she ate Oreos as a kid: dropping them into a glass of cold milk, catching them with a fork before they hit bottom, then popping them into her mouth whole. She told me of dreamy child-hood New Year's Day journal entries and about her brother and his crazy, "fatal attraction" girlfriends. The image of my budding friend becoming a viable, promising Republican presidential candidate crystallized.

In exchange for her stories, I shared the time my brother and I got our tongues stuck to the swing set after a neighbor's evil dare, how I used to judge the pool-basketball-dunks of my cousins and brother, and of the time Rob dragged olympically uncoordinated me, like a rag-doll, through a high-ropes course.

Though we were just scratching the surface of memories, I could feel our friendship banging into being. As our lives intersected and created new memories, we were getting to know each other...and ourselves...more deeply. In my core I felt that if Margie ever needed a friend, I'd be there for her. I sensed she felt the same way about me. Being around her brought out the best in me. She was a mirror in the sun, daily reflecting ways to be more fun, more like Christ, more honest and daring, more open and centered, more holy.

One of my most fond collegiate memories of Margie happened my senior year and Margie's junior. It was the night of our cho-rale's Christmas concert during which, as a music major, I had the privilege and pain of conducting a trio of pieces. The pieces were in multiple meters, and I felt inadequate in following the score. Worried I would trip across the stage, completely get lost in the notes, or butterfinger the baton, I reluctantly and fearfully invited all the women with whom I shared a house to the concert. Margie was one of them. The entire evening felt like an out-of-body experience. The only grounding force was seeing Margie, along with the others, in the front row. With eyes sparkling from anticipation and cheerleader smiles, they willed me to do well. Their presence fortified me to grip the baton, wave it at the correct tempo, show dynamics and cut-offs, and even stay stalwartly in rhythm amid battling duples and triples.

After the concert, feeling relieved, I headed to our house hoping to celebrate with my friends. Walking up snow-covered steps, I noticed that every window was dark. Feeling like the "cheese standing alone," I sat down on our family room couch, resting a heavy, disappointed head in my hands. Cold fingertips touched my forehead, palms supported my cheeks. *Where was everyone? Would my victory go unnoticed, uncelebrated?*

Within minutes I heard stomping on the front stoop accompanied by laughter. In came Margie like a gust of winter wind, hands bursting with a bouquet of red roses. Behind her were the rest of my friends holding the strings of helium balloon bouquets and congratulatory cards! Margie knew how much this evening meant to me and exactly what I needed: to know that I lived in a loving, supportive sisterhood. She'd rallied all our girlfriends and threw an impromptu party for me—replacing my feelings of aloneness with festivity, writing a celebratory line into the story of my life.

Since that day, Margie and I have stood beside each other in a handful of weddings, grocery store lines, parties, and mom's groups. Whenever we're together, I expect the storyline of my life to take unexpected twists and turns, revealing rich truths about myself and the world.

Recently Margie asked me to be with her and her husband, John, for the birth of their second child, Josiah. I asked Margie exactly what she needed. She wanted me to pray, massage her lower back, and take pictures. "But," she warned me, "absolutely *no* crotch shots!"

During the labor and delivery, I gave my valiant friend honor, respect, and lots of ice-cold Coke. I also ignored her photographic admonitions. She'd let me in on a sacred moment, allowing me to see the rapturous, vivid, precarious entrance of new life. In return, I wanted her to see it too. So planning on asking for forgiveness instead of permission, I clicked several Ansil Adams' exactly as Josiah emerged.

When I gave Margie the photos, thankfully she didn't kill me. As it turned out, one of her favorite birth memories are my pictures. She loves studying them, seeing the way John tenderly caught fresh-from-God Josiah and noticing the glistening umbilical cord that still tied her to their babe.

Our friends celebrate us and we celebrate them, seeing ourselves in ways we never could on our own.

> *Our friends come to us in waves: at work, in the library, at parent–teacher nights. Some of these friendships are massively important, and some simply get us through the day. I've drawn the conclusion that taken together they help us fill in the blanks, they give us a purpose. Because all friendships are finally mirrors.*[2]
>
> BETH KEPHART

God's Word—*Completing the Pages of our Lives*

> *O LORD, you have searched me and you know me.*
>
> PSALM 139:1

> *God did indeed send his only begotten son to come and*
> *live with us...to help us understand our stories—each*
> *one unique, infinitely valuable, irreplaceable.*[3]
>
> MADELEINE L'ENGLE

God's Word has an uncanny way of cutting to the very core of us, knowing our secrets, our desires, our every detail—even when we can't see ourselves clearly. Often when we read the Bible we feel like its pages fill in missing parts of our life story with truth, comfort, healing, stories of others like us, and grace. Perhaps one reason we sometimes shrink back from reading Scripture is because being fully known feels simultaneously beautiful and painful, exposed and understood.

Just like Margie, we don't want to have revealing photographs taken. We don't want to admit we need each other. We hide from the truth about ourselves. But once we do take a look, we're freed by the stunning, breathtaking truth of knowing, sharing our needs, and seeing the whole story. Whether read from the pulpit, under a tree in the park, with friends at Bible study, or under a quilt in bed, God's Word has a marvelous way of magnifying our stories...of celebrating us and letting us see ourselves clearly.

When we let it, God's Word fills in the blanks of our lives. It becomes a mirror in which we see ourselves clearly. Sometimes when a situation appears as murky as a mud puddle, or when we feel alone needing direction and hope, the Author and Perfecter gives us a good word from His Word (Hebrews 12:2). I've paraphrased a few passages that have done this for me so you too can experience peace.

In Times of Fear

Don't be scared even in shadowy places. I am God. I am in charge. Wherever you go, I'm with you—overseeing, protecting, guiding, loving. Don't panic. I am God. I'll give you strength and help, ideas and opportunities. When it seems like your safety net is fraying, I'll scoop you up in My gentle-but-calloused hands and hold you.

Remember, when you're held in My love there's no room for fear. My love around you is so big it doesn't leave even a molecule of space for worry or anxiety. The only time fear comes is when you think punishment's ominous, nefarious shadow follows you. I am God—a God of love. I don't want to hurt you; I want to fulfill you through love. Let Me gently catch you, show you who you are, and who I'm making you to be: one perfected in My love (Psalm 23:4; Isaiah 41:10; 1 John 4:18).

In Times of Hoping

Why are you feeling down? Do you feel as if some of your hopes and dreams have soared into the sky like a bright-red balloon...only to pop under the ozone's pressure? I see your hopes. I know your story. I know the desires of your heart. I want to fulfill them and to fulfill you. When you are feeling exhausted and deflated, know that My plans are to make you feel as buoyant as air.

I also want to ground you with a soul anchor, firm and secure. I will plant your feet and dreams in fertile soil where they can take root and grow to the heavens (Psalm 42:5; Proverbs 13:12; Isaiah 40:30-31; Hebrews 6:19).

In Times of Labor

If you let me, I'll make you happy in your work. Please celebrate your accomplishments. Savor them. Stop striving and enjoy the moments: each diaper you change, word you type, dish you wash, painting you paint, client you serve, document you mail, invalid you nurse. See that I am with you in daily life, making your work fruitful and giving you joy for the journey. I celebrate the simple-yet-profound victories with you.

Be sure to offer the duties of your day to me because I'm the one who gives you the hands and heart and will to work. When you feel you can't towel up another glass of spilled apple juice, stay patient with toddlers, tackle a megalith of bills, or pursue your dreams, know that I remember your work and the love with which you do it. Continue to help My people (Deuteronomy 16:15; Ecclesiastes 5:19; Colossians 3:23; Hebrews 6:10).

In the same way that Margie and I have seen each other, become mirrors to each other, filled in each other's blanks, so can God's Word. When we open the Bible, some of God's handwritten words perfectly fit the mad-lib blanks in the stories of our lives. The words help us see ourselves, our memories, our lives in ways that espouse hope and help. Just as an editor's pen untangles jumbled manuscripts, so God's words scribble sense into our messy, mixed-up days. When we feel alone, God's words remind us that He's buying us roses. And when we really don't want to look, His words will give us positive views of ourselves we never dreamed of seeing.

> *O Lord, you have searched me and you know me. You know when I sit and when I rise;*
>
> *You perceive my thoughts from afar.*
>
> *You discern my going out and my lying down;*
>
> *You are familiar with all my ways...*
>
> *All the days ordained for me were written in your book before one of them came to be.*
>
> *How precious to me are your thoughts, O God!*
>
> *How vast is the sum of them!*
>
> Psalm 139:1-3,16-17

Our Word—*Scriptures, Insights, & Suggestions*

1. If any of the paraphrased Scriptures particularly touched you,

take a moment to look up the actual verses. Read them over several times. Let their truths sink in and fill in any blanks you have in your mad-lib life right now.

2. Is there a friend who has been a particularly good mirror to you? Write her a note of gratitude. Tell her what she has revealed to you about yourself.

3. Is there a biblical passage that is a mirror to you? If so, reread the passage and paraphrase it in your journal.

4. Choose a sentence from one of the epistles, the psalms, or one of the Gospels that is a mirror to you. Write a one-page journal entry about how it reflects in your life.

> *We are to stand alongside our friends,*
> *entering into their passionate struggles and trials and*
> *triumphs, feeling their pangs of pain and the brimming*
> *over of their pleasure. Mirroring back to them, some-*
> *times, their better selves, when they need our affirmation*
> *and encouragement. Giving them permission to mirror*
> *back to us our less attractive attributes, so that we can...*
> *work on personal transformation, with God's help.*[4]
>
> LUCI SHAW

Unexpected Friends

The Bible, a Book of Surprises

*Friends bring light, love, mercy, and grace to one another
in simple, ordinary, sometimes unexpected ways.*[1]

SALLY MILLER AND CHERI MUELLER

Her Word—*Cheri's Bert to my Ernie*

Cheri and I are as different as the moon and sun. She's an introvert; I'm an extrovert. She likes to work on one project at a time; I
try to juggle a dozen. She tends to be concealed and quiet; I tend
to be bold and boisterous. She's catlike. I'm more like a slobbering,
overzealous canine. She reminds me of *Sesame Street's* Bert. I'm
more like Ernie. We laugh as we identify ourselves with people in
the media. Just the other day Cher said, "I'm Oprah. You're Gale,
constantly singing, chasing hamburgers, and dreaming."

Whenever Cheri and I are asked to share an appearance at a
women's conference or gathering, Cheri inevitably winds up telling
the story of how we met.[2] The story perfectly points out our alter-
ego personalities and usually provides fuel for a little laughter.

First Cheri paints a picture of herself and her sweet, Southern
belle roommate, Laurie, nesting in their cocoon of a room. They're
fluffing comforters in quiet, sticky-tacking posters to the wall in
peace, organizing dresser drawers with the tranquility of monastic

practitioners under a vow of silence. *Until* (and she always adds a pregnant pause after the "until")...*until*...the settling in was interrupted by a "boisterous, operatic voice that came bouncing and bellowing through the small corridor of a bathroom that linked [her] to [her] suite mates."

This voice belonged to me, and I can't contest the fact that it still tends to be operatic, boisterous, and bellowing. Cheri continues the tale by describing the way she and Laurie, "without saying a word, tentatively approached the trumpeting voice."

O.K., I can go with operatic, boisterous, and bellowing. But I think Cheri crosses a line with "trumpeting." (For the record, though, Heather, Margie, and several of my other friends side with Cheri on the issue.)

I guess the worst part of the story of our meeting comes next. Cher, no-holds barred, describes what she *saw* when she turned that life-changing corner. "A girl with long, jet-black hair who wore fluorescent pink lipstick and a pearl-beaded, turquoise jumpsuit..." I agree with the hair and the lipstick (it *was* the 80s). But I protest the turquoise, pearl-beaded jumpsuit. I *did* wear lots of turquoise and had a few jumpsuits, but pearl-beaded? Come on!

The funny (and slightly heartwarming) thing is that over Cheri's and my 20 years of friendship and dozens of retellings of this story, I've come to visualize myself in a pearl-beaded, turquoise jumpsuit on the day I met my lifelong friend. It's also heartwarming to remember the marrow-deep longing I had to make new friends on that historic day at Wheaton College. And even more thrilling when I realize God saw the desire of my heart and gave it to me in a shy, introverted girl from Minnesota who ended up being wiser, deeper, and more insightful, honest, gracious, close to the heart of God, and creative than anyone I've ever met.

Cheri would say that it took years for us to understand each other's rhythms. (Probably because getting used to a trumpeting suite mate *would* take a bit of adjusting.) But I felt at home with Cheri right away. Though her ability to be still, her acquaintance with life-giving grace, and her introspective nature felt foreign and surprising to me, I wanted to learn from Cheri, to befriend her, to walk through life with her.

Since that day at Wheaton, Cheri and I have sung songs and read Scriptures at each other's weddings. We've supported each other through five pregnancies and one adoption. We've served as godparents to each other's children. We've written a handful of books and read and talked about hundreds more. And with each interaction, our oppositeness brings depth, meaning, and hilarity we never could've anticipated.

As I reminisce about our meeting, its unexpected nature doesn't shock me anymore. I love the fact that Cheri and I have been foils of a sort from the get-go. And today I embrace the ways Cheri's unique perspectives, insights, and ideas continue to baffle, cajole, challenge, and surprise me.

God's Word—*Surprised by God*

I closed the Bible, feeling the deep click of truth that comes when God reaches out in startling ways from its pages. We seem to think that God speaks by seconding the ideas we've already adopted, but God nearly always catches us by surprise.[3]

SUE MONK KIDD

God never ceases to amaze me. His ways are higher than my ways (Isaiah 55:9). He's done surprising, unexpected things in my life and throughout history. When the world was expecting God to visit in the form of a conquering king, He came as a defenseless infant, born of a virgin, in a tiny village called Bethlehem. Who would have ever imagined that?

Now, as we look for Christ to return, we reflect on apocalyptic passages in Revelation, imagining once again the approach of a conquering king. We read Revelation 19:11-13: "I saw heaven standing open and there before me was a white horse, whose rider is called Faithful and True. With justice he judges and makes war. His eyes are like blazing fire, and on his head are many crowns... He is dressed in a robe dipped in blood, and his name is the Word of God."

Though some of the images in this passage suggest war and pillage, they also name Christ as "Faithful and True," and "the Word of God." Are we anticipating the return of a war-loving God? Perhaps we're stuck in the Old Testament, embracing images of a crusader God out to punish instead of offering grace.

Perhaps we'll be surprised to see how Christ returns. He will surely fulfill prophecy: coming and redeeming in power and complete control. But I think the predictions we've conjured fall far short of the glorious creativity, the higher ways, the unexpected surprises the Rider on the White Horse has up His blood-soaked sleeve. Just as He came in a surprising way the first time, so will His return comfort and confound.

Just yesterday I was in a Bible study. We were talking about the astonishing nature of God and some of our astounding findings in Scripture. One woman shared, "I was so shocked to read of King David, the psalmist and man after God's own heart, having an affair. I think of him as so holy. I had a hard time stomaching this part of his story."

I confessed that I'd a similar moment of freaking out when I read the passage about Noah being naked and drunk in his tent (Genesis 9:21). For my entire life, Noah had been the long, white-bearded man with the staff, herding all the earth's animals in pairs onto a boat. He was a holy man, chosen by God to build an ark against the weatherman's prediction of sunny skies. It shocked me to find him two-sheets-to-the-wind and indecently exposed.

Another woman in my group noted, "The entire book of Genesis is about a dysfunctional family." Laughter erupted. We went around the table sharing our unexpected discoveries: Cain killing Abel (Genesis 4:8). Abram lying about Sarah being his sister (Genesis 12:12,19). Jacob gypping Esau out of his birthright and becoming the father of a nation (Genesis 27).

"Isn't God surprising?" I asked. The circle of women nodded. God lets wholly human (or holy human) people—just like us—be His story, do His work, receive His love. We also agreed that His ways and weavings are usually countercultural, and they can sometimes seem counterintuitive. We commented on the way *we* would have "done Old Testament history" vs. the way God did it. And we pondered the confounding nature of the cross. One woman mentioned that Paul says God's wisdom often looks foolish to humans (1 Corinthians 1:27).

When I went to Wheaton College almost 20 years ago, I expected to meet people a lot like me: interested in music, a little loud, off-center, and boldly clinging to spiritual law. I had it all planned out. Instead I met Cheri, a woman whose gentle spirit taught me to be still, to live in the moment, to abide in Christ, to receive grace.

When we open the pages of Scripture, we often read with preconceived notions. We expect to find words and people who fit in with our predispositions about faith and holy living. "Cookie-cutter Christians" who don't smoke, drink, or swear. Instead we find David in bed with Bathsheba (2 Samuel 11–12), Saul supping with the witch of Endor (1 Samuel 28), Peter, one of Jesus' best friends, cutting off the ear of a Roman soldier (John 18:10).

In the mix, God is present like an alchemist: melding people and circumstances together for His ultimate glory and good (Romans 8:28). Isn't it amazing how God uses everyday, broken, flawed, sin-soaked people—people like us—to reveal His golden, glorious godhead? We never know how God is going to show up! For me, He has come in the gentle, introverted, so-different-from-me face of Cheri. And He has come for all of us in the astonishing truths of Scripture.

Our Word—*Scriptures, Insights, & Suggestions*

1. Do you think of God as predictable or surprising? Why? How does this fit with biblical truth?

2. What are your expectations of the Bible?

3. How has God's Word surprised you recently?

4. Are you open to God's Word challenging predispositions you have about faith and holy living? Why or why not?

> *If it's God's Spirit blowing, someone ends up having feathers ruffled in an unforeseen way.*
> *God tends to confound, astonish, and flabbergast.*
> *A Bethlehem stable, a Roman cross, an empty garden tomb. We might as well reconcile ourselves to the fact that God's truth often turns up in ways we don't expect.*[4]
>
> SUE MONK KIDD

18

Expectant Friends
Waiting with the Word

*Slowly, steadily, surely, the time approaches when the
vision will be fulfilled. If it seems slow, wait patiently, for
it will surely take place. It will not be delayed.*

HABAKKUK 2:3 NLT

Her Word—*Cheri's Rose Picture*

There has been no other time in my life when I was more
keenly aware of being in waiting than when I was pregnant. I
guess that's why women are called "expectant" when they're with
child: expecting growth, expecting life, expecting pain and beauty.
During my first pregnancy I obsessed over fetal growth, creating
a calendar covered with glossy photographs taken inside a laden
womb. "Today our baby can hear" or "today our baby can suck
his thumb," I'd excitedly report to Bryan with each flip of the calendar.

Friends, family, and strangers frequently reached out to rub my
bulbous belly and ask when my due date was. When I told them it
was January 3, 2000, they either freaked out about a Y2K hospital
disaster or said how special it would be if our baby was born on the
first day of the new millennium. I wasn't worried about Y2K, I was
too busy waiting to meet the little one who was a melding of my
chromosomes and Bry's.

As any woman who has ever been pregnant knows, there is

waiting. And then there is *waaaaiting*. *Waaaaiting* occurs during the last few weeks of pregnancy when you feel like an alien has moved into your body, inhabiting and enlarging not only your belly, but your hands, nose, feet, and butt as well. You fantasize about a stunt double showing up for the remaining days of gestation and definitely for the birth. Your abdominal skin is stretched so tightly you know it will chronically sag once the alien is ejected. You imagine your distended belly button as the pop-out thermometer on a Thanksgiving turkey. When your husband makes a turkey-related reference, you consider committing an act of hormone-induced homicide.

On December 31, 1999, I was *waaaaiting*. I remember making a batch of double chocolate brownies in an effort to spur the birth process on. I also watched a dozen episodes of *A Baby Story*. My hope was that the combination of chocolate and watching birth after birth would start something rumbling within me.

That evening Bryan and I went to his sister's for a New Year's Eve dinner. All through the appetizers and salad, I was experiencing abdominal pain. I had to leave the room to manage it. *This couldn't be it, could it?* Suddenly even after all the *waaaaiting*, I was scared that my day of deliverance might have arrived!

At 4:02 AM—after a sleepless night—Bry and I were admitted to the hospital. I was devastated to find out that after ten hours of labor, though I was 100 percent effaced, I was only one measly centimeter dilated. A nurse determined that I was feverish, stuck an IV in me for hydration, and informed us that there was a chance my contractions would subside and she'd have to send me home. *Send me home?* Tears welled up in my eyes. *Send me home? I thought this was it! And now I might have to bear the humiliation of being sent home with no baby.*

Just as tears started rolling in hot, salty streams down my cheeks, Cheri walked into the hospital room. In her presence I felt free to let out the dismal sobs that had been lurking in my chest. Breathlessly I told my friend what the nasty nurse said. Cheri quickly took off her coat, walked to my bedside, and grabbed my swollen fingers in icy-cold hands. The coldness was soothing. I noticed she smelled of snow from the January outdoors. I deeply inhaled the fresh aroma.

With passion in her green eyes and pupils dilated in conviction, Cheri looked squarely at me and said, "You're not going anywhere. *This is it!*" My friend had walked with me through weeks of expectant anticipation and the eager, exhausting *waaaaiting.* She knew my time was ripe. With three words she assuaged my worries and refreshed my spirit.

Bryan and I were both glad to have Cheri with us during the last few hours of expecting Ben. She walked the hospital corridors with me, pushing the IV. She prayed for me. And when I wasn't progressing, she gave me a metaphor—like good writers do—to help during my contractions.

"Picture your cervix like a rose, opening up with each wave of pain." It sounds a little silly (and Cheri hates it when I tell this part of the story). But her image *really* helped. As I write about it now, I think of the way Cher's words gave me a measure of grace and helped move me toward change...just like she does in a million other areas of my life.

Because Cheri walks with me, waits with me, gives me just the right, imaginative, life-giving words at perfect times, God births new things in me. Some days He births patience, kindness, or creativity. And, on January 1, 2000, at 2:37 PM He birthed 8-pound, 11-ounce Benjamin Bosch Miller. Hallelujah!

God's Word—*Simeon's Expectant End*

> *The Bible is rich with language urging us to wait.*
> *If you want to be impressed, note how often*
> *God's people seem to be waiting.*[1]
>
> SUE MONK KIDD

There was a man named Simeon, a righteous and devout Jew, who lived in first-century Palestine. He was expectant too. Simeon was looking for the fulfillment of one of God's amazing promises. The Holy Spirit had revealed to Simeon that he would "not die before he had seen the Lord's Christ" (Luke 2:26).

I have a vivid picture of Simeon in mind. He hangs out near the temple *waaaaiting* for news. He paces, wrings his hands, runs his fingers through his coarse, white beard, behaving much like fathers in delivery waiting rooms. His brow is furrowed. His mind is focused so deeply on the promise he's been given that he appears distracted, preoccupied, even bumbling. His body is old with aching joints and creaking bones. He longs for Zion, and rest, and ultimate healing. But he keeps his vigil knowing God will not offer that rest until his cataract-covered eyes behold the Christ.

I imagine that one day, just as Simeon was about to pluck a fig off a tree outside the temple courtyard, a stiff breeze caught his attention. It was not any old breeze. It was cold, clear, and powerful, swirling wherever it wanted to go. It whispered truths in the ears of anyone who would listen. Simeon sensed the Holy Spirit in the wind. It moved him into the temple courts.

There he saw what he had been waiting for: the baby Jesus. Adrenaline coursed through his body like lightning. He wanted to run, to shout, to click ancient heels. Instead, with reverence and gentleness, he approached Mary and Joseph. With teary and twinkling eyes, he outstretched grandfatherly arms toward the babe. As she did with stinky shepherds, sojourning wise men, and noisy angels, Mary obliged him.

Simeon held his long-awaited promise—our long-awaited promise—in his arms. The moment must have been as momentous as the first time I held Ben in my arms: transcendent and holy, yet fully organic. Overtaken by emotion, Simeon prayed, "Sovereign Lord, as you have promised, you now dismiss your servant in peace. For my eyes have seen your salvation, which you have prepared in the sight of all people, a light for revelation to the Gentiles and for glory to your people Israel" (Luke 2:29-32).

Simeon's waiting was over. The world's waiting was over. He gave the baby back to his mother and walked out of the temple. His hope fulfilled, his thirst slaked…a man completed and readied for rest.

When we open up the Bible, we find dozens of God's people waiting like Simeon. Jonah waits in the sloshy innards of a whale. A father waits for his empty-pocketed son's return. The disciples wait for their dearest friend to rise from the dead. Simeon waits for the Word to arrive in an unexpected bundle…the baby Jesus. The true Word became flesh, dwelling with us, making the *waaaait* worth it. Cheri waited with me. She gave me encouraging words while I waited. Anytime we have to wait, we have the characters and words of the Bible to companion us, to give us perspective, hope, and refreshment. Besides, reading God's Word is always a great thing to do while waiting!

Our Word—*Scriptures, Insights, & Suggestions*

> *I wondered if waiting was the "missing link" in spiritual evolving, the lost and forgotten experience crucial to becoming fully human, fully Christian, fully ourselves.*[2]
>
> SUE MONK KIDD

1. What is your relationship with waiting? Why?

2. The next time you're waiting in line at the grocery story, at a red light, or at a train or bus stop, notice your posture in waiting. Are you anxious and impatient or peaceful and expectant? Does this reflect your ability to wait in other, perhaps bigger, areas of your life?

3. How can you practice peaceful waiting at times of transition in your life? Perhaps taking a deep breath, a drink of water, or talking to God will help. Try one of these the next time your day is feeling frenetic or overwhelming.

4. Meditate on and memorize these verses about waiting: Psalm 27:14; 130:5; Isaiah 30:18; Romans 8:23; Titus 2:13.

When important times of transition came for Jesus, he entered enclosures of waiting—the wilderness, a garden, the tomb. Jesus' life was a balanced rhythm of waiting on God and expressing the fruits of that waiting.[3]

SUE MONK KIDD

19

Freedom Within Boundaries

The Bible as Creative Parent

Children's reactions are unpredictable.
You never know which gesture, tradition, or offbeat,
spur-of-the-moment adventure will become a
"little thing long remembered"—embedded happily and
fondly in their minds forever.[1]

SUSAN NEWMAN

Her Word—*Brynn's Watermelon and Jail Visit*

In *With Child,* Phyllis Chesler's exquisite, articulate diary of motherhood, she writes, "I'll search for Mothers, dead and alive, to guide me. In dusty manuscripts, in new anthologies—in my living room or theirs." I, along with Phyllis, am an explorer in search of Mother-guides. Thankfully, I've found them in books, like hers, and in my living room. Brynn is one of those guides. She's a creative, energetic girlfriend and mother of five. I'm inspired by her inventive ways of connecting with, teaching, and nurturing her brood.

On a firefly-speckled evening this summer, Brynn displayed her dazzling parenting. After warning her two oldest boys to take a samurai sword fight from their bedroom to the basement, Brynn went to clean a nearby bathroom. The brothers ignored their mom, continuing the fray, and within minutes the oldest boy pushed his little brother toward an open, second-story window. The four-year-old crashed against the screen, which catapulted to the grassy ground far below. The assailant rushed toward his brother, who was gripping the window molding for dear life. He managed to pull him back to safety.

White-faced and shaking, the brothers found Brynn kneeling by a porcelain throne. She was clad in rubber gloves and holding a scrub-brush scepter. After hearing their tale of disobedience and near death, Brynn later confessed to me that she nearly committed imperial homicide. Instead she used her anger as fuel for creative parenting.

What can I do to be sure this never happens again? she asked herself.

I laughed when she told me that, for some strange reason, a watermelon popped into her head. She retrieved one from the fridge, took the boys back to the scene of their crime, and asked what they thought would happen if she threw the melon out the bedroom window. The boys took turns thumping the great fruit and then each other's skulls. In a hands-on, hollow-sounding, didactic moment, they imagined the demise of the hydrocephalic husk.

Before the boys could comment further, Brynn projected the melon. It shocked the little ones and confirmed their hypothesis in a juicy, pink-and-green splat.

"David Letterman would've been proud," I told my friend.

She laughed and said her little swordsmen haven't played samurai in their room since.

Recently Brynn and I were talking about the ways we might educate our children about drugs. I wasn't surprised one iota when she shared yet another innovative parenting plan. When her children reach the appropriate ages, she plans on taking each of them on a field trip to a drug rehab center and a local jail. There she'll have them tour the facilities, interview residents, get a taste of the consequences of drug use. Her babes will have tangible, visible reasons to just say no.

In the thick of mothering, when I'm feeling frustrated by my kids' disobedience and I'm sick of reminding them to say "please and thank you," put away their toys, stop whining, and come when they are told, I think of Brynn. I visualize the ways she lovingly disciplines. Instead of yelling, she redirects. Instead of nagging, she consistently reinforces disobedience with consequences. Instead of preaching with pious pomposity, she lives a life of gentleness, playfulness, creativity, and grace.

Lovingly, vividly, profoundly Brynn is giving her children healthy roots along with the incredible opportunity to sprout wings and fly. She is teaching, directing, and disciplining with structured boundaries. These boundaries allow her brood to feel loved, protected, cared for. Inside her fence of family rules is the freedom to run and grow and play. As she adds each picket, her little ones develop a sense of belonging, of being loved. And they learn how to make wise choices that will ultimately let them leave through the gates and establish their own safe and spacious places.

God's Word—*Loving, Merciful* Disciplinarian

> *No discipline seems pleasant at the time, but painful.*
> *Later on, however, it produces a harvest of righteousness*
> *and peace for those who have been trained by it.*
>
> HEBREWS 12:11

I feel a little queasy as I write this chapter. I'm not comfortable with discipline. I didn't like it as a child. And as an adult, with some sense of liberation, I find it even less palatable. The thought of getting a time-out from the Trinity, being "grounded" by God, or getting some kind of supernatural "spanking" scares me.

When I casually read Hebrews, chapter 12, I found myself worrying that a patriarchal, war-loving Old Testament God was waiting with angry eyes to catch my every peccadillo. I even worried that writing about discipline would—in some crazy way—make me vulnerable to God's punitive penchant.

The funny thing is that as I *studied* Hebrews 12 and Ephesians, chapter 6, verse 4, I discovered that Paul wanted the recipients of his letters to "avoid the heavy-handed, physical brutality practiced by their pagan neighbors. Discipline was not to evoke anger from the children."[2] The God of the New Testament lives and moves and relates with us based on a New Covenant, a new deal. Christ comes and chooses to receive the ultimate punishment for my sins (and yours!), and then you and I receive unthinkable, unimaginable grace. In His New Covenant with us, God is a loving disciplinarian who advocates the kind of creative, growth-espousing discipline Brynn practices.

As I read Hebrews, the even funnier thing I realized is that as adults we have a choice of whether or not we embrace God's discipline. That may sound strange, but in the psalms, David wrote that God puts His laws before us (18:22). David turned toward those laws, and we too have that choice. We can close our Bibles, let them collect dust on our shelves, and do life our own way. Or we can explore the growth-producing, countercultural, challenges presented in the parchment pages. Yes, it can be frightening to sit down with an open heart and flip open the Bible. We never know what we may find: a new perspective, a dare to step out, or the scariest thing ever: mercy. (Sometimes we run from God because we're in a cycle of self-punishment. Turning toward Him stops that cycle and exposes us to the truth about ourselves and then to the tenderizing gift of grace. Crazed, relentless grace—a love that doesn't let go—can be almost as frightening as punishment.)

When we turn toward the Book and its unpredictable, turn-us-upside-down words, we become *disc*iples and God becomes our *disc*ipliner. It frees me to know that the word *discipline* comes from the Latin root *disco,* meaning "to get to know, learn, or have a direct acquaintance with." Discipline is not limited to punishment. It encompasses a way of life. It refers to the process of willingly becoming God's *disciple,* willingly getting to know Him by listening for His voice, reading His Word, letting go of our own stratagem and allowing God to take us into the labyrinth of His love.

Though this life-altering process is not meant to be abusive in any way, it can be painful. Humans find it hard to let go of our white-knuckled grip on how we want life to be. But I encourage you to do so! When we turn ourselves and our wills over to daily, divine direction, God doesn't come down on us in a raging fire. He whispers to us in the wind and shows us the way through stories, songs, epistles, family, and friends.

Like Brynn, He drops watermelons into our wrestlings and invites us to visit uncomfortable places like jails and rehab centers. His goal is not to confine, break, or hurt us. It's to mold, refine, and birth us. God, like any good mother, guides our journey so we always end up in satisfying pastures of long, succulent, green.

> *He brought me out into a spacious place;*
> *he rescued me because he delighted in me.*
>
> PSALM 18:19

> *Scripture is true. Truth is deeper and wider and*
> *much more demanding than many people would like,*
> *but Jesus promised that it would set us free.*[3]
>
> MADELEINE L'ENGLE

Our Word—*Scriptures, Insights, & Suggestions*

> *It is very easy to grieve the Spirit of God; we do it by despising the discipline of the Lord, or by becoming discouraged when He rebukes us...When the Lord disciplines you...let Him have His way with you. Allow Him to put you into a right-standing relationship before God.*[4]
>
> OSWALD CHAMBERS

1. What is your relationship with your parents? How do they impact your relationship with God?

2. Have you experienced God as parent? What kind of Father and Mother is He?

3. Read Hebrews 12 and Psalm 119:45. Consider your view of discipline. Do you see it as punitive or relational? Why? How does your view affect your understanding of the Bible and your willingness to consider becoming a *disc*iple?

> *My [daughter], do not make light of the Lord's discipline, and do not lose heart when he rebukes you, because the Lord disciplines those he loves, and he punishes everyone he accepts as a [daughter].*
>
> HEBREWS 12:5-6

20

Soul Spa
God's Rejuvenating Word

[The LORD] leads me beside quiet waters,
he restores my soul.

PSALM 23:2-3

Her Word—*Girls' Spa Retreat*

My fortieth birthday is approaching like a freight train. Almost daily I imagine the girlfriend get-together I hope to have to celebrate this rite of passage. Early this morning I was perusing one of my favorite spa resort websites to consider party options. The site opens with music enhanced by the sounds of gently rushing water, rain sticks, tender pianissimo drums, sonorous finger cymbals. The beautiful images captivate and mesmerize. My shoulders melt into the back of my rocking chair as I take in towering, bottle-green pines beside oceanic turquoise pools. Women clad in white terry-cloth robes and towel turbans rest with bare feet and exhibit serene smiles. Some of them sit beside a pool sipping rehydrating, detoxifying potions from tall, crystalline glasses. Others lie relaxed on massage tables under the skilled, strong, tension-releasing hands of professional masseurs. Candles radiate soft halo auras and scented oils line countertops in tidy rows. Regeneration calls like a friend.

Suddenly my oasis balloon pops. My children are rustling

in their beds. Soon I hear three pairs of feet rushing down the hallway in a crescendo, targeting my writing room. *I will not rush,* I admonish. But I have to speed-read to take in every welcoming word scrolling on the page before my brood breaks in and shatters my serenity. *We invite you to...energize your soul.* (I hear one of the children whining. I inhale deeply. Before I can exhale, it sounds like he's pushing his brother against the wall. A brawl is breaking out.)

A beautiful escape for body and spirit...arising from nature to lift your soul. (The baby starts clamoring. She's saying something about "num-num" and "ba-ba.") *A place of wellness and well being. Tranquility.* (A brouhaha is definitely going on in the hallway. It's rolling toward me like a tornado. I consider getting up to intervene but the stormy trio fills my doorway.)

"What are you doing, Mommy?" asks my middle child. I pretend I don't hear him in an effort to read the last few words of tantalizing text: *Rejuvenation. Pure joy. Where we invite you to inspire your spirit. Live in harmony.* While I read, the baby is using my hair as a grappling rope with the hope of summiting my lap.

"What's that cool music?" my oldest child asks as he tries to box-out his brother and squeeze closer to the computer screen.

"Oh, it's nothing," I say as I hug all three babes and shuffle them out of my room and down to the kitchen for breakfast.

While I stick waffles in the toaster oven, the boys fight over who gets to hold the Spiderman comic I left on the table for them. During their battle I mentally drift back to the spa. I picture an uninterrupted, long weekend with my three closest friends. I can practically feel Margie's welcoming hugs, hear Heather's quippy jokes, and imagine Cheri's fresh and wise insights about midlife. I relish the thoughts of time with friends accompanied by laughter and the texture of joyful voices.

Much later, during my daughter's naptime, I return to the health resort site. This time I explore spa cuisine. The menu is vast, eclectic, mouth-watering. For breakfast: grilled wheatberry toast with cinnamon, yogurt, cheese, organic raspberry jam, apples, and sunflower seeds. Lunch: a grilled vegetable labyrinth, grilled tuna rolled in a sun-dried tomato flatbread with Boursin herb cheese and Romaine lettuce and served with blue corn chips and seasonal fruit (Yum!). Dinner: jumbo shrimp, veggies in a spicy Sambal with organic salad greens, grilled flatbread, green tea quinoa. Also available is a vegan entrée of specially prepared tofu.

I can practically taste the spices and hear my friends and me as we share equally savory conversations. That the cuisine had been featured in *Travel and Leisure* magazine didn't impress me nearly as much as the fact that *I* didn't have to prepare the food. My friends and I would be able to feast and talk, talk and feast uninterrupted.

I clicked on *Girlfriends' Spa Therapy Package* and was examining the options: radiant glow organic facial, aromatherapy, signature pedicure, marma massage. The phone clanged. It was Heather. When she asked, "Whatcha doin'?" I told her.

Together we sighed and dreamed about temporarily escaping the clamor and chaos of motherhood, rejuvenating with exercise, body treatments, healthy food, heart-to-hearts. Just fantasizing about the spa relaxed, renewed, restored, refreshed, and readied us to face the world once again.

God's Word—*A Spa for the Spirit*

> *I urge you, [sisters], in view of God's mercy, to...be transformed by the renewing of your mind.*
>
> ROMANS 12:1-2

Clearly not all women want to spend a weekend at a spa. Cheri would rather be on a horse-riding adventure or on an artsy-fartsy escape. Whether we enjoy being pampered or not, purifying bath rituals, massages, body wrappings, manicures, and facials are perfect metaphors for the ways meditating on God's Word refreshes and restores our souls.

Purifying Bath Ritual

My favorite spa describes their proprietary purifying bath ritual as a self-guided treatment designed to cleanse the skin and clear the mind. First, guests step into an oversized shower with a rainfall showerhead. Sandstone Body Polish is used to exfoliate and prepare skin for the application of a nourishing body mist, followed by an aroma steam. Then a second rinse in a rainfall shower cools down the system before guests soak in an essential oil-enhanced hot pool with massaging jets.

After luxuriating in this description, I can't help but think of a passage in Phillip W. Keller's *A Shepherd Looks at Psalm 23*. According to Keller, to protect their sheep from flies, scab-disease, and other pests, shepherds "completely submerge [each animal] in an oil solution until its entire body is soaked." This strikes me simultaneously as humorous and beneficent. I can just see those struggling shepherds fighting and wrestling stubborn sheep into a bath that will ultimately protect them.

I would have to do something similar myself! I imagine getting my slightly overweight, middle-aged body into a communal shower to be exfoliated, oiled, heated, and cooled. I feel vulnerable and intimidated. Standing in my swimsuit, dripping wet, isn't my first choice as a great weekend starter. But it will prepare me for the rest of the spa experience. And if I abandon myself to the process, it will feel good and *be* good for me. Can you relate?

Sometimes opening the pages of Scripture feels just as vulnerable and self-exposing as stepping into a spa shower. God has a way of using His Words to exfoliate, soften, and, ultimately, soothe our souls. This process often means jettisoning our own plans for a better plan. Other times it means releasing anger against a husband, friend, coworker, or family member. Spiritual growth in our lives can be demanding, surprising, evocative of change, and challenging. So it may feel easier to avoid the pages altogether than to plunge in, get wet, and soak until we're soft. But never forget the outcome...lives and spirits that are sweet to the Lord and those around us!

Massage

Most spas offer a variety of massages. Therapists typically customize treatments for clients. A masseuse may choose Swedish, aromatherapy, hot stone, or other methods. Techniques range from fans, circles, spine snakes, back circles to trapezius squeezes, tendon valleys, tendon squeezes, and forearm slides. Each focuses on increasing circulation and inducing deep relaxation to provide stress relief and healing.

When we take a moment to sit down with a cup of green tea and have an hour of quiet with the Bible, God's words have a therapeutic way of rubbing out some of the knotted, tense, sore spots in our spirits. Knots of worry are kneaded with this assurance: "Do not be anxious about anything, but in everything, by prayer and petition, with thanksgiving, present your requests to God. And the peace of God...will guard your hearts" (Philippians 4:6-7). Tensions from carrying heavy burdens at work or at home melt away under the strong-yet-tender words of Jesus: "Come to me, all you who are weary and burdened, and I will give you rest" (Matthew 11:28). Sore spots in our relationships are massaged with, "Be patient, bearing with one another in love. Make every effort to keep the unity of the Spirit through the bond of peace" (Ephesians 4:2-3). When we get off the divine masseuse's table we feel realigned, centered, able to move with ease and grace through our days.

Body Wrap and Scalp Massage

The spa I hope to one day visit offers a chocolate mousse body wrap that is deliciously hydrating. First comes a cranberry body scrub. This is followed by a sour cherry and Hungarian cocoa body mask. While the mask is working its magic, the esthetician performs a face and scalp massage. Chocolate (with no calories). Peace. Quiet. Massage. What could be better!

When I imagine my girlfriends and me experiencing the chocolate mousse body wrap and scalp massage I laugh a little. I guarantee one or more of us will be tempted to taste the treatment. But just like coffee, it'll probably smell a lot better than it tastes.

Picturing this encompassing treatment brings to mind 2 Corinthians 2:14, which describes the knowledge of Christ as a fragrance that permeates everything. I think of the ways I've gotten to know Christ through my friends and the way memorizing verses and passages of Scripture has helped me get to know God better. (On particularly frenetic days it's comforting to connect with God through verses I carry in my mind, my purse, or my pockets.)

Memorizing Scripture is like having a masseuse massage grace and truth into our heads. Then she wraps our entire bodies in the sweetness, wonderful aroma, and healing mask of words that are good and true. Words that are "sweeter than honey, than honey from the comb" (Psalm 19:10). If we allow these words to be infused into our bodies, they become part of who we are, how we talk, where we go, what we desire.

Manicure

A truly lavish manicure begins with a relaxing hands soak in scented water. Next is an exfoliation using natural sea salts and aromatherapy oil. A relaxing massage with moisturizing lotion leaves hands silky and smooth. The massage is followed by a cooling mud mask to soothe and detoxify skin. The final touch is a choice of buffing or polishing the fingernails.

The Bible is replete with images of hands: Christ's nail-pierced hands (Psalm 22:16), the trees of the field clapping their hands in praise to God (Isaiah 55:12), a woman extending hands to the needy (Proverbs 31), God holding out His hands to an obstinate people (Isaiah 65:2).

As a wife, mother, and writer, my hands are precious to me. I want to be sure that they are open in submission and relinquishment. I want them ready to praise and ready to touch the needy with hope, and help, and healing. Though a good manicure beautifies my nails and relaxes muscles, nothing can better prepare my hands for their work than turning the pages of Scripture.

Hair Removal, Facial, and Makeup

A radiant glow organic facial is a naturally healing treatment that restores what the stresses of life take away using ancient remedies of herbs and fruits. The formula is customized for each client and addresses the concerns of premature aging, sun damage, sensitive skin, and combination skin. It provides a healthy glow and rejuvenated skin. Organic ingredients include wild plum, sour cherry, lemon, grape, and paprika. After the facial is a massage and a deeply penetrating healing mask followed by hair removal (if necessary) and a cosmetic makeover.

My girlfriends and I will conclude our weekend of spa heaven with facials. We'll take the archetypal pictures of each other—faces covered in green glop save for two raccoon-circle eyes. Then three of us will be off to cosmetic makeover land. One will be left behind for an excruciating upper lip and brow wax.

I wanted to avoid spilling this beauty bean, but the fact of the matter is that *I'm* the one who'll be left behind. I've been trying to hide it for years but I can grow a mustache faster than my hubby. Needless to say, my girlfriends will probably be halfway through foundation and eyes before the esthetician even begins taming my black-rooted beast of brows and upper lip.

When we're all finally beautified: lips pinked, cheeks blushed, eyes enhanced, worry lines relaxed, we'll gather our bags and head home. During the first few seconds after our arrival home, our families will notice our radiance. I doubt they'll compare our faces to the glowing countenance Moses had after summiting Mount Sinai to meet face to face with God, but surely they'll notice *some kind* of difference.

As I think about time with my radiant-faced friends I realize that manicures, facials, makeovers, and body wraps will be a blast! But even without these beauty treatments, my friends are truly beautiful...soul deep beautiful. Their spirits shimmer each time they share a favorite passage with a friend, encourage their kids with a Bible story, write an apropos verse at the end of a love note. Beauty creams, rouge, and eye shadow will never replace the gorgeousness grown from years of reading, poring over, meditating on the rejuvenating, restorative, refreshing Word of God.

> *The LORD their God will save [his people]...*
> *They will sparkle in his land like jewels in a crown.*
> *How attractive and beautiful they will be!*
>
> ZECHARIAH 9:16-17

Our Word—*Scriptures, Insights, & Suggestions*

> *Ask where the good way is, and walk in it,*
> *and you will find rest for your souls.*
>
> JEREMIAH 6:16

1. Pamper yourself this week. Take a long bath. Do your nails. Gather some girlfriends and get a pedicure together. Enjoy receiving rest for your body and spirit.

2. Exercise three or four (or even more) times this week. Do something you enjoy: hiking, swimming, a spin class, snowshoeing, lifting, yoga, canoeing, dance. Thank God for the way your body moves and feels and how that directly affects your soul.

3. Focus on creating or purchasing a healthy meal (perhaps a "vegetable labyrinth"—whatever *that* is—or something as simple as a salad from McDonald's). If you feel short on ideas, visit one of my favorite websites: www.hungrygirl.com. Notice the way your body and soul feel after honoring God through healthful eating. Journal about this if you feel so inspired.

4. Experience a spiritual spa. Go someplace where you can be uninterrupted: the library, a park, a friend's empty house, a restaurant, a hotel, a retreat center. Take your Bible, a journal, a pen. (You may also want to bring art supplies, music, edifying books.) Ease into the day. Sit quietly before God with your coffee (or green tea) and Bible. Ask for guidance. Listen. Read. Write. Pray. Sleep. Dream. Paint. Dance. Be exfoliated, massaged, purified, beautified by your time with the Word.

*We, who with unveiled faces all reflect the
Lord's glory, are being transformed into his likeness
with ever-increasing glory, which comes from
the Lord, who is the Spirit.*

2 Corinthians 3:18

21

Dream Catchers

Absorbing Truth Even as We Sleep

> *For some time I had been coming to appreciate and understand how dreams...contained revelations and symbolic images opening us to a deeper spiritual realm.*[1]
>
> SUE MONK KIDD

Her Word—*Grabbing the Tiger by the Tail*

When my husband and I returned from China with our adopted baby girl, I had the strangest dream. In the first scene of the dream, I was at the Gloria Plaza in Nanchung. As I entered the revolving door, I was expecting to rescue a spotted, wobbly legged fawn that I noticed in the hotel lobby. As the door spun and I walked through, the fawn metamorphosed into a baby lion, roaring and toothy. I felt scared, worried, baited-and-switched.

Looking back as I got to know the spicy, sassy little girl God had given to Bryan and me, it doesn't take a dream analyst to explain these images. It is obvious I had imagined our daughter being a gentle, needy fawn, coloring in her coloring book on the fringes of our lives. But when I met Ling XuRan, she was more like a baby lion: playful and independent (even at the tender age of 12 months), entering our lives with ferocity and a roaring presence.

Cut to the next scene of my dream. I was in a bus with our two boys. On the bus we rode with windows wide open, hair blowing like tall grasses on the savannah. Fear overtook me again as I noticed an enormous, muscle-bound mama lion racing toward the back of our bus, snarling, baring fangs, extending claws. My sons cowered in fear. I assured them they were safe. In a gravity defying feat, the lioness bounded into the bus through the back window. On her way toward me, she gashed my oldest son's forehead. Ben began to bleed profusely, looking at me with coal-black eyes of disbelief and heartbreak.

In an act of superhuman strength, I fought the beast, successfully throwing my son's attacker out one of the bus' windows. As the cat plummeted to the road racing below us, I noticed I had come out of the fray unscathed. I also saw the lioness metamorphosing into a striped being. *A tiger?* I wondered. Then a Bible verse flashed in my mind: "By His stripes we are healed" (Isaiah 53:5 NKJV).

The dream confounded me. I didn't understand the second scene. It weighed on me during waking moments. I was tormented. I knew the lioness in the dream represented me. And I was deeply saddened to think I had caused my son such deep and irrevocable pain.

A few days after having the lion dream, I went to Minnesota to see Cheri. She had recently had a wallop of a dream too. She shared it with me over lunch at McDonald's. Even in the afterglow of her vulnerability with me, I was afraid and embarrassed to reciprocate. I was so ashamed that I dreamed of wounding Ben. But I so badly wanted Cheri's help to unravel the symbolic images. Halfway through our salads, I finally cut through my defenses, broke down, and spilled the dream. Without missing a beat Cheri said, "We're all human. We make mistakes. And we sometimes unavoidably hurt our kids, Sal."

I began crying into my Coke.

She continued. "As a mother lion, you can be fierce, strong, and playful. Don't feel bad about who you are. Just decide when to extend or retract your claws."

I cried harder.

"I've watched you care for your 'cubs'—protecting them, teaching them, nurturing them in the wildness of living." Her gracing words simultaneously hurt and healed. "You're doing a good job, Sal, even if you don't fit into some preconceived maternal molds."

My Coke was getting more saline by the minute. As a mom, I had often been wary of my strong and potentially hostile personality. I didn't think it fit in with the gentle nurturing nature I imagined "good" mothers having.

The dream and Cheri helped me see that the fierce, angry lioness that wounds can be transformed into an equally strong tiger, protecting and playing with her young in strength and beauty. I know that I'll never be a mother doe, parenting with a mild, calm, moderate placidity. (And Emily will never be a fawn. She needs the spunk and spryness of a baby lion to provide resiliency for the pains associated with adoption.) Remembering my dream helps me integrate my wild-woman personality into my nurturing, protective mom role.

This week I've been preparing for Emily's second birthday. We're throwing a "Moon Yuet" party in Chinatown for her. As I prepare for the celebration, I've been pulling out a few souvenirs we brought home from China almost one year ago. I found a miniature jade bracelet, a tea set, and a silk dress. I also discovered a pair of traditional, bright-pink and green Chinese Tiger Shoes embroidered with red floss. *Tiger Shoes, Tiger Shoes, Tiger Shoes,* I repeated in my mind. On her birthday, Emily will be wearing *tigers* on her feet. I smiled knowing that in China the shoes symbolically represent protection for a baby's first steps.

God's Word—*Wisdom of Dream and Dreams of Wisdom*

> *In the Bible, dreams are one of the most significant*
> *ways through which God communicates.*[2]
>
> SUE MONK KIDD

It's uncanny the way dreams come into our lives at transitional times. I think they often give us glimpses of God's thoughts. They propel us to look at our lives, nurture change and growth, and usually elicit creative movement in our beings. One of my favorite authors is C.S. Lewis. He has a way of giving just the right words to my faith experience. This year I've been reading his children's book series *The Chronicles of Narnia* to my boys at bedtime. They're fascinated with any scene featuring Aslan, the mighty lion and Christ figure of the series. When asked how he came up with Aslan, Lewis notes that while writing the Narnia books he began having dreams about lions. With fervor he adds, "Aslan bounded in." Lewis' accounting brings new depth of meaning to the phrase *"I dreamed it up!"*

In Old Testament times God often communicated through dreams. Joseph was a dreamer (Genesis 37, 40, 41). Daniel was a dreamer and interpreter of dreams (Daniel 2, 4, 7). God even talked to Abimelech (Genesis 20) and Pharaoh (Genesis 41) through their dreams. In the New Testament, Joseph, Jesus' earthly dad, had a dream that made him Christ's adoptive father (Matthew 1:20). Pilate's wife "suffered a great deal...in a dream" because of Jesus (Matthew 27:19). How I'd like to know what *that* dream was about!

One of my favorite Old Testament dream weavers is King Solomon. In 1 Kings 3, we find him deep in a demonstrative dream. During the dream, God appears to Solomon and says, "Ask for whatever you want me to give you" (verse 5).

If I were in Solomon's shoes, I would have had a heyday. Or

maybe I would've just had a hard time narrowing down my requests: Manolo Blahnik shoes, a home makeover, a new wardrobe (including sparkly accessories), a successful writing career, literary awards, the guarantee for a long, luxurious, pain-free life…Oh, how unlike King Solomon I am. Instead of getting emerald-eyed with gargantuan greed like me, Solomon makes some reverential comments to God—honoring Him and acknowledging His faithfulness to King David, Solomon's father. Then Solomon says, "Your servant is here among the people you have chosen, a great people, too numerous to count or number. So give your servant a discerning heart to govern your people and to distinguish between right and wrong" (verses 8-9).

Wow! Solomon identifies himself as God's servant twice in this short passage and proves his servitude by asking God for something that will ultimately serve and reflect God—a discerning heart! In the dream God says, "Since you have asked for this and not for long life or wealth for yourself…I will do what you have asked. I will give you a wise and discerning heart, so that there will never have been anyone like you, nor will there ever be" (verses 11-12).

In the following passage, 1 Kings 3:16-28, King Solomon is presented with a problem during his waking life. Two young mothers are arguing over a baby boy. As prostitutes, they live in the same brothel. During the night one of the women rolls on top of and suffocates her baby. She then sneaks into her coworker's room and swaps her lifeless son for the breathing babe. In the morning mayhem breaks loose and both women claim to be the living baby's mother. They soon find themselves at the foot of King Solomon's newly broken in throne.

In a cool, calculated move, Solomon asks for the baby and a hair-splittingly sharp sword. Then he commands, "Cut the living child in two and give half to one and half to the other" (verse 25).

Of course, the woman whose son is alive is filled with a fierce lioness dose of maternal compassion and pleads, "Please, my lord, give her the living baby! Don't kill him!" (verse 26).

The other woman says, "Neither I nor you shall have him. Cut him in two!" (verse 26).

When Solomon gives the baby to the first woman, it becomes eminently clear to all of Israel that Solomon is wise indeed. His nighttime request for wisdom has obviously been granted.

I find it of tantamount import that Solomon asked God for wisdom in his dream. And I think it's even more important that God gave the gift of discernment to Solomon as he slept. How often do we believe we have to work our way to wisdom, gritting through spiritual life with guts and gumption? Then God surprises us and does dream work with us as we sleep. Amazing! Wispy, image-laden night pictures can, and often are, harbingers and heralds of wisdom.

As we read of dreamers in the Bible and have our own nocturnal imaginings, let's be open to the truth and wisdom God sheds on us like gentle moonbeams. Let us be restful as He completes the good work He began in us (Philippians 1:6). And when we open our eyes to read His Word, let's be calm, quiet, and still enough to let truth come bounding in!

> For God does speak—now one way, now another—though [woman] may not perceive it. In a dream, in a vision of the night, when deep sleep falls on [women] as they slumber in their beds, he may speak in their ears.
>
> JOB 33:14-16

Our Word—*Scriptures, Insights, & Suggestions*

1. Do you have any recurring dreams? Write them down. Ask God to help you see what the symbols mean.

2. Before you fall asleep tonight invite God to speak to you in your

sleeping hours. When you awake, be prayerfully aware of any dreams you may have had.

3. Read about Joseph interacting with dreams in Genesis, chapters 37, 40, and 41. Which of the dreams stands out to you? What does the dream mean to you? Write a poem or journal about it or take a walk and consider it.

4. In the same way the lion came bounding into my dream and Aslan came bounding into the subconscious of C.S. Lewis, what is bounding into your dreams? Why?

> *In the last days, God says, I will pour out my Spirit on all people. Your sons and daughters will prophesy, your young men will see visions, your old men will dream dreams. Even on my servants, both men and women, I will pour out my Spirit in those days.*
>
> ACTS 2:17-18

22

God's Garden
The Bible as Botanical

*We wander among divine daffodils framed in a
lacework of crab apples and along forget-me-not paths
disappearing into flowery glades.*[1]

TOVAH MARTIN

Her Word—*Billie's Bee Balm*

For over a decade I've been intoxicated by my mother-in-law's
garden. Almost every time I go to Billie's home we take a walk
through her perennial beds, her wild flowers, and her vegetable
gardens to see what new plants are poking green heads up through
the stubborn Illinois clay.

The walk begins as we pass beneath an aromatic arch garlanded
in vines of tiny white roses. We continue toward Billie's perennial
border that stretches in a serpentine amble along an edge of emerald
grass. Hostas, looking like huge, variegated spiders, complement
bulbous purple alliums. Gangly verbenas dance beside brilliant blue
patches of borage. Billie laughs as she notices feverfew, cleome, and
Johnny-jump-up "volunteers," which she points out to me.

Next to the playhouse, a vortex that sucks in my children and
their cousins, is the wild garden. It's a colorful cauldron of cross-
pollination, photosynthesis, and growth. Cosmos bloom, a hops

vine climbs up the trunk of a dead tree, and raspberry stalks tangle. Billie and I pick handfuls of berries. They're tart and seedy on our tongues.

We're still enjoying the summery aftertaste while we meander toward the vegetable garden. A barn birdhouse is this area's focal point. It towers over heirloom tomatoes, leeks, a tepee of scarlet runner beans, and some carrots. Hollyhock giants, guarding the rows of veggies, show off colorful blooms for the bumblebees and us.

Whenever Billie and I go on a garden walk, we take our time. Billie deadheads a few plants, and I ask her what a few others are called. We amble and admire, examine and explore. Time almost stands still when we're in her garden. Beauty, growth, and the fruit of hard work are our companions. It is a good place to be. A holy place.

When Bryan and I were first married, Billie came to our new home with several pots, bags of soil, and herb seedlings. Not being an experienced gardener, I did my planting of the pots in the middle of our kitchen floor. Needless to say, potting mix made its way like already-chewed-gum in the sole of a sneaker into all the crevices of the kitchen tile. I discovered that gardening is definitely an outdoor activity!

Years later Bryan and Billie helped me plan and execute a small rectangle vegetable garden in our backyard. Unfortunately, gardening and my bad back didn't make good bedfellows. By the end of the summer hideous weeds choked out my radishes, carrots, sweet peas, and cantaloupe vines, leaving only a huge, gangly patch of zucchini that threatened to overtake our entire neighborhood.

These days when I want to experience a garden in full glory, I go to Billie's. There I get lost in the lilacs, dazed by the daisies, enchanted by the echinacea, and bedazzled by bee balm. Every time I do, it dawns on me that Billie's garden is her church, her sanctuary. It's where she meets with God.

In the soil and foliage, my mother-in-law encounters meaning and purpose. During her artistic designing, catalog ordering, trips to the botanical society, planting, replanting, weeding, and pruning, she encounters the divine. She walks with God during the cool of the day in her garden.

> *The man and his wife heard the sound of the LORD God*
> *as he was walking in the garden in the cool of the day.*
>
> GENESIS 3:8

God's Word—*Walking with God in the Green*

> *God is, of course, the first to have designed a garden...*
> *God chose the site, planned and planted it himself, with*
> *people in mind. He walked there and sought intimate*
> *companionship there with the people he had made.*[2]
>
> JOYCE SACKETT

I've always found it interesting that the Bible begins and ends in a garden. In the beginning, God walked with His first kids in the Garden of Eden, where He planted the Tree of Knowledge (Genesis 1). And in the end, He grows another tree, the Tree of Life, beside a crystal river (Revelation 22). This tree has healing leaves and yields a crop of fruit every month.

In many biblical passages between the two trees, God uses gardening images and metaphors to teach and enlighten. In Luke 12 Jesus teases His closest buds about their worrying. He asks them to "consider the lilies," to watch how they grow. To take in their beauty and realize that though they shoot up from the soil where their bulbs landed, even King Solomon didn't have raiment as lovely as theirs!

I can just imagine Jesus walking through vineyards, farmlands, and home gardens with His pals. The growing things in the surroundings probably inspired the Teacher to share life-changing, paradigm-shifting ideas with His sometimes numskulled, nature-loving friends. "I am the true vine, and my Father is the gardener" (John 15:1). "The truth is, a kernel of wheat must be planted in the soil. Unless it dies it will be alone—a single seed. But its death will produce many new kernels—a plentiful harvest" (John 12:24).

Whether or not the disciples "got it" and knew Jesus was the vine and the kernel didn't completely matter. Christ planted seeds of truth into the hearts of His friends just as He plants seedling truths into our hearts. Every time Jesus and the disciples sat by a fire, questions were discussed and stories were repeated. Seeds germinated. Sprouts emerged. Growth occurred.

Every time I take a garden walk with Billie, I notice something new, vibrant, breathtaking. The walks nourish numskulled, nature-loving me...a woman a lot like the disciples. The same thing happens when I open the Bible.

Reading God's Word and truly listening to Jesus' voice are like spending time in the garden. I take meandering journeys and embrace new discoveries with each step. Truths tower and dance around me like golden-yellow coreopsis. Scrawny characters and unpredictable plot twists challenge my preconceived notions like the "volunteers" in Billie's perennial border. And with every page turn, I walk with God in the cool of the day.

Our Word—*Scriptures, Insights, & Suggestions*

> *May your roots go down deep into the soil of God's marvelous love. And may you have the power to understand, as all God's people should, how wide, how long, how high, and how deep his love really is.*
>
> Ephesians 3:17-18

1. Do you have a garden? Is it a holy sanctuary where you can meet with God? Why or why not?

2. If you have a garden, plant something new. As it germinates, grows, and goes to seed, make notes in your journal about the process. Are there any soul connections?

3. If you don't have a garden, plant something in a pot and observe its growth. (Based on personal experience, I recommend potting outdoors!) Observe the growth and changes in your new plant. Journal the process. Notice any soul-growing connections.

4. What is your favorite place in the world? What do you enjoy about this place? What do you experience here? How has God met you and walked with you here?

5. Was it helpful to consider enjoying a garden walk as a metaphor for reading the Bible? If yes, take a walk through a garden and meditate on God and His wisdom.

Today, in our fast-paced, hectic world,
a garden can provide the relief our soul needs. It can
provide a place to be quiet, to think and seek God's
presence. Even a window ledge where we have greenery
can become for us a retreat. We can draw up a chair,
sit and enjoy the freshness of our plants, and relax. We
can keep our Bibles near that window garden and make
it our meeting place with the Lord.[3]

JOYCE SACKETT

Sustaining Meals

The Bible as Daily Bread

> *God makes us as broken bread and poured-out*
> *wine to please Himself.*[1]
>
> OSWALD CHAMBERS

Her Word—*Lilah's Peppermint Hot Fudge*

The menu was delicious: Spicy Chicken Enchiladas, Freshly Chopped Salsa with Cilantro, Peppermint Ice Cream with Home-made Hot Fudge. Absolutely DE-LI-CIOUS! Lilah made the meal. She hand delivered it, along with a huge hug, days after my hubby and I returned exhausted and jet-lagged from China's JiangXi Province with our daughter.

Our circle of friends has a tradition of catering luxurious meals for one another when anyone in the group gives birth, is hospitalized, has a sick loved one, moves, or—as in my most recent scenario—experiences an adoptive journey. This tradition lightens the load of grocery shopping and meal preparation. And, more importantly, it allows us to stay connected, sustain one another during crises, and truly be Christ's body, broken, for each other.

Today it was my turn to bring a meal to Lilah. I packed my favorite picnic lunch (which I first prepared for Cheri when she brought her firstborn home from the hospital). The menu: Lemonade, Chips, a Veggie and Swiss Cheese Sandwich served on a Baguette with Dill Sauce, and Thin Mints for dessert. Everything fit perfectly in a heart-shaped basket.

The synchronicity of packing the lunch in a heart dawned on me as I wedged mums into the basket's top, right lobe. Heart-shaped was how the surgeons had described my friend's uterus two days earlier. They told her the baby she'd carried for five months had wedged himself into the uterus, and when he didn't descend, the womb ruptured.

My friend's baby, the surgeon noted, didn't have to be extricated from his vascular nest in an impassable and necessary attempt to stop the bleeding. He'd already been expelled and, in a severe mercy, died instantly. My friend's life was still in peril, though. Her blood pressure dropped like a stone into a pond. Only through multiple blood transfusions did it begin to rise again.

The second I heard Lilah was pregnant with her third child, I planned on making my postpartum picnic. I never dreamed I'd be doing it four months too early with Sadness as my sous chef.

I was shaking as I reached into my fridge for the dill dressing which, when added to my basket, would complete the fare. In a shelf on the door I noticed the bottle of homemade hot fudge Lilah had made for me just a few months ago. I started to cry. It struck me as strange and wonderful the way the women in my circle of friends have prepared and received meals of help and celebration. We trade roles of caterer and guest; one season being bread, the next being broken.

Through give and take over the years, I realized that though we've been feeding each other fine cuisine, the true feast is our friendship. During difficult moments we've been together, prayed for one another, listened, and shared. In caring, crying, and making sandwiches we nourish each other in ways more satisfying than the grandest food.

The process of being made broken bread and poured-out wine means that you have to be the nourishment for other people's souls until they learn to feed on God.[2]

OSWALD CHAMBERS

God's Word—*Bread from the Heavens*

Give us this day our daily bread.

MATTHEW 6:1 NASB

The Bible is filled with stories of God bringing daily bread, being broken bread for His people. One of my Old Testament favorites takes place in the desert, and one of my New Testament favorites happens on a grassy hillside.

In Exodus, chapter 16, we find the Israelites exhausted and bedraggled from their romp through the Red Sea. Hungry, they grumble. Their stomachs rumble, and they fantasize about "pots of meat" they used to eat in Egypt.

God sees their hunger and promises Moses, "I will rain down bread from heaven for you" (Exodus 16:4). Manna. Hotcakes from heaven. It fell from cumulous clouds, satisfying God's children.

Years later we find Jesus standing on a hillside with His best friends. A hungry crowd of 5,000 gathers, waiting for a word. Jesus asks the multitude to sit in the grass while He supersizes a little boy's lunch into a mega meal. For hours Jesus and His pals distribute the multiplying loaves.

Three things strike me about this story: 1) The gatherers come hungry, hurting, asking for help and hope. 2) Jesus' only requirement of them is to sit in the grass. 3) There is an abundance of leftovers.

The hillside squatters and the desert wanderers remind me of my friends and me. At different times we're all bedraggled, hungry, exhausted, wounded from life's unexpected punches. We cry out to each other and to God for sustenance. And He answers by giving us hot fudge, homemade by our friends, and His Word.

Sometimes His Word hits the spot as much as the hot fudge satisfies our sweet tooth. It brings us stories that, much like my friends' meals, sustain, fortify, and nourish. As we read we realize the Bible is daily bread leavened by the wisdom of God's words. And it becomes ever so clear that "[woman] does not live on bread alone but on every word that comes from the mouth of the LORD" (Deuteronomy 8:3).

Scripture alone is not enough to slake our hunger. Just as the meals of my friends without their love and companionship would leave me longing for more, so it is with reading the Bible. Unless we feast on the companionship of Christ, our grumblings will continue.

I don't think it was coincidental when this week I picked up my bright-orange Bible and read Jesus' words, "It is not Moses who has given you the bread from heaven, but it is my Father who gives you the true bread from heaven. For the bread of God is he who comes down from heaven...I am the bread of life. He who comes to me will never go hungry" (John 6:32-33,35).

Our Word—*Scriptures, Insights, & Suggestions*

> *Friends give nourishment of all kinds to one another.*
> *We sustain one another. In so many ways we offer*
> *to one another the feasts of our friendship.*[3]
>
> MADELEINE L'ENGLE

1. In what ways have your girlfriends been "broken bread and spilled out wine" for you? In what ways have you been the same for them?

2. Think of one of your best dining experiences. Does reading the Bible remind you of this experience? Why or why not?

3. In your journal make four columns. At the top of each write: the name of a friend, The Bible, Christ, and your favorite meal. Next make a list of how each column topper entity sustains your life daily. What similarities or differences do you discover?

Home

The Bible Dwelling in Us

*I want to go wherever you go and to live
wherever you live; your people shall be my people,
and your God shall be my God.*

RUTH 1:16 TLB

Her Word—*Mrs. Olsen Filling in the Blanks*

One thing I tenaciously value in this life is being with friends during rites of passage: births, deaths, weddings, other celebrations. I believe Christ is palpably present in the tender times of transition—when we're full of feeling, open to hugs, yearning for sisterhood. Whatever the cost, I try to heartily partake of these moments.

Margie and I were with Cheri praying right before the emergency C-section that brought forth her first child, Jennifer. I recalled the hours Cheri had walked circles in the hospital with me, pushing my IV bag, and ultimately vehemently demanding the anesthesiologist administer my epidural before my first son, Ben, was born. Likewise, when our books are born, Cheri and I celebrate with dinners, cards, gifts. When Margie's husband was diagnosed with brain cancer I rushed home from an out-of-state trip and went straight to her house with an embrace, a prayer book, and a pint of Rocky Road.

Last week when I got a call from Heather who shared the news that her mom, after suffering for several years with Parkinson's-related disease, had died, I knew I had to pack a bag, cut a family vacation short, set aside the writing of my latest book for a few days so I could go to my friend. I worried about my husband and kids. I worried about my rapidly impending deadline. But ultimately I trusted that making the sacrifice to be physically present at the funeral would end up blessing my family, my friend, and even my book.

The chapel was overflowing with flowers, grandchildren, and Longaberger baskets stuffed with candy (many of the baskets had been hand-painted by Heather's mom, Mrs. Olsen). A legacy of photographs adorned the place with the warmth and luminescence of lit dinner candles. Near the coffin, bright in a lilac-colored sweater and the dazzle of vulnerability, I saw Heather. I slowly approached her, a dubious feat for bold, boisterous me. We squeezed each other hard. During the embrace, our tear-wet cheeks brushed. I thought it apropos that our tears combined.

"Do you want to take me to her?" I quietly asked.

Heather nodded.

We approached the open casket. "Mrs. Olsen!" I wanted to cry out, as I often did when she greeted me at the door of her home, at collegiate concerts, at family reunions, at baby showers. Instead I smiled and whispered her name. I noticed her lovely lavender-and-slate-blue blouse and wondered if Heather had chosen it. I looked at the necklace resting on her chest. It was laden with birthstone bejeweled charms representing each of 12 grandchildren. Her fingernails and lips were rose-petal pink. "She looks pretty," I said.

Heather shared that though she thought her mom's hair looked pretty and it was a comfort to see the hands normally held in fists due to the disease finally at rest, the vestige didn't seem like her mother.

I thought about my last visit with Mrs. Olsen. I'd packed towers of music and my old electric keyboard into my minivan and trekked to her Wisconsin nursing home apartment to share songs and memories. After hugs and a half hour of duets with Heather, I worried that I was overstaying my welcome and exhausting my gracious hostess. I asked, "Have you heard enough, Mrs. Olsen? Are we wearing you out with all this racket? Or would you like to hear more songs?"

From her wheelchair, Heather's mother stretched her neck forward like a baby bird and, with every ounce of energy and will she could muster, breathed out a gruff, "Mmmmooohhhhhhrrrre... sssssssooohhhhhnnnngs." These two words were the only words she spoke during our visit. And they were the last I'll ever hear Mrs. Olsen speak this side of heaven.

At the funeral, Heather and her siblings shared more final and precious words. Along with these were stories threaded with strands of Carol Olsen's hospitality, creativity, generosity, easily recognizable and ready laughter, love for her valiantly devoted husband and family. Heather shared one story that I will never forget.

"Recently," Heather began, "I visited Mom. I noticed a wooden box of Scripture memory cards that Rachel, my sister, had sent. I casually picked up the box and started flipping through the cards. Following a gentle prompting, I began reading the words of some familiar verses aloud. As I read, I deliberately left out key words. 'Those who hope in the Lord will renew their strength. They will soar on wings like...'

"In the silent space, Mom filled in 'eeeeaaaagles.' Verse after verse, she filled in the blanks."

I sat in the chapel's tenth row, listening to Heather's story, looking at pictures of Carol Olsen—alive, pretty, vibrant, smiling. I imagined the days when she led Bible studies in her home and days when she lingered in God's Word—meditating, memorizing, treasuring the Scriptures during still moments while her children were at school or in bed. I thought about the ways the Word was with Carol her entire life. The Word dwelt richly in her even during the last difficult and draining days. I cried jubilant tears realizing that years of God's Word dwelling in her perfectly prepared Mrs. Olsen for her current deep and delightful home.

Surely goodness and love will follow me all the days of my life, and I will dwell in the house of the LORD forever.

PSALM 23:6

God's Word—*Our Dwelling Place*

Let the word of Christ dwell in you richly.

COLOSSIANS 3:16

I love the idea that we can dwell in the Word, and it can dwell in us. It's a great place to be when we can't presently reside in the complete, utterly lovely, mind blowing presence of God. To tide us over for heaven, we can dwell in the Scriptures and, by doing so, soak up God and His presence.

Time and again Scripture mentions that God is our dwelling place and our portion forever. In Psalm 91:9 and 10, King David writes, "If you make the Most High your dwelling—even the LORD, who is my refuge—then no harm will befall you, no disaster will come near your tent." I like thinking of our home here as a tent, a temporary place to live while our permanent digs are being prepared.

The Bible also says we are God's dwelling place! In Ephesians 2:22 Paul notes, "In him you too are being built together to become a dwelling in which God lives by his Spirit." Isn't that paradox intoxicating? Just as we abide in God, He lives in us!

The Greek word for dwell is *katoikeō*. According to *Vine's Expository Dictionary of New Testament Words, katoikeō* is "the most frequent verb...meaning...to settle down in a dwelling, to dwell fixedly in a place." This word can be found in Philippians 4:8: "Finally, brethren, whatever is true, whatever is honorable, whatever is right, whatever is pure, whatever is lovely, whatever is of good repute, if there is any excellence and if anything worthy of praise, *dwell* on these things."

Mrs. Olsen knew how to do this. As she made Pfeffernusse cookies, Snackers, and the surprisingly delicious sandwiches concocted with peanut butter, Miracle Whip, and November tomatoes, Scripture in colorful calligraphy by Timothy Botts hung beside her on kitchen walls. As she named delphiniums and daisies, heliotropes and hostas on her walks, she knew that the "earth is full of God's creation" (Psalm 104:24). Scriptures indwelt her mind even when she was sick and unable to walk or cook. No matter where Carol was or what she was doing, God and His Word were with her, taking residence in her.

Like her, I want to dwell deeply in the Scriptures so when I reach my final dwelling place it will feel like being home.

Now the dwelling of God is with men,
and he will live with them. They will be his people,
and God himself will be with them and be their God.

REVELATION 21:3

Our Word—*Scriptures, Insights, & Suggestions*

1. What was your childhood home like? Draw a picture or write a description of it. Was it a warm, inviting place filled with soft places to sit, good things to eat, beautiful things to see?

2. How does your experience with "home" affect your understanding of God as your home? Write about this.

3. What does it mean to you to "abide" in Christ (John 15:4 NASB)?
   Do you feel like you currently dwell in the Scriptures? Why or
   why not? Pray Colossians 3:16, actively encouraging the word
   of Christ to dwell richly within you.

> *If anyone loves me, he will obey my teaching.*
> *My Father will love him, and we will come to him*
> *and make our home with him.*
>
> JOHN 14:23

Eyes
The Bible as a Way to See Christ

*Let us fix our eyes on Jesus, the author
and perfecter of our faith.*

HEBREWS 12:2

Her Word—*Cheri's Picture of Jesus*

Cheri's eyes have always fascinated me. She has writer's eyes...
seer's eyes. They're big and round and deeply green, the color of
the sea. When she gets really intense about something her pupils
dilate, almost completely blackening. Sometimes I study her long-
lashed eyes and wonder if their loveliness is one of the reasons Cheri
always sees beauty and profundity in the world around her. I also
wonder if her *particular* eyes help her see Christ in a clear, unob-
structed, face-to-face reality.

This has dawned on me during several occasions. Our sophomore year in college Cheri had a graphite sketch of Christ hanging
over her bunk. I found the piece atrocious. It focused intention-
ally, almost microscopically, on the face of the dying Christ. The
work was contorted, asymmetrical, almost pop-art in style. Christ's
crown was twisted in a tortuous arc—almost in 3-D. His eyes, tear
heavy, looked like they belonged to two different people. They were
placed precariously on the face mimicking Van Gogh style.

Cheri's roommate wanted her to take the piece down. Cher protested, feeling attached to the art that had been sketched by a friend from home. I, the mere suite mate, dared not weigh in on the subject. Instead, I thought about Cheri's bond with the picture. She was willing to have a poignant, graphic, daily reminder of God's Passion, of His willingness to relinquish control. Cheri lived in an open-handed place, letting go of things that I held on to with white-knuckle intensity. I wondered if she saw something in the picture I was unable to.

Our senior year I had a similar experience with Cheri. We went to a campus production of *Godspell*. Sitting side by side in theater seats, we took in scene after scene of a playful, poignant, accessible, even rambunctious Jesus. He wore rainbow-striped suspenders with ripped blue jeans and somersaulted across the stage. He told jokes to modern-day fishermen friends, comforted a sultry Mary Magdalene with song, and high-fived John the Baptist.

This new theatrical approach to the Gospels was irreverent, invigorating, and refreshing. After more than a decade of walking with Christ, I felt in that moment like I was getting to know Him in a new way. It scared me. I didn't know how to interact with this demonstrative venue. I turned toward my friend. Her eyes were wide, pupils huge. She was bedazzled, rapt, crying. Her tears granted me permission to see Christ in this new way.

Recently Cheri and I were parlaying a passage in the New Testament—Matthew 5, to be exact. The Beatitudes. I had just completed a Sunday school class examining this particular passage. My well-meaning teacher indicated that each of the "blessed" qualities: poorness in spirit, mourning, meekness, hungering and thirsting for righteousness, should be "put on" in the form of disciplines. This sat strangely with me. I wondered if this teaching was metamorphosing gifts into laws. I shared this with Cheri, and she agreed. Then, with unique perspective, she added, "I can just *see* Jesus on the hillside. I imagine Him looking into the eyes of various wounded, brokenhearted people. I'll bet He knew some of them intimately enough to be aware of their personal journeys. Others He probably sized-up through intuition and wisdom."

I sat back in my overstuffed chair expectantly, waiting to hear more of Cheri's view.

"This may sound crazy," she continued, "but I imagine Christ looking deeply into the eyes of a woman who recently lost her husband and saying, 'Blessed are those who mourn, for they will be comforted.' Or maybe He noticed a group of women who had been following Him from town to town and said, 'Blessed are those who hunger and thirst for righteousness, for they will be filled.'"

"I think you're on to something, Cher," I said. We continued playing out scenarios for all of the "Blesseds." As we did, I knew Cheri's pupils were completely large and dark with just a sliver of glimmering green around the edges of her irises.

Blessed are the pure in heart, for they will see God.

MATTHEW 5:8

God's Word—*A Portrait of Christ*

Another misconception is of Jesus as a sad, self-pitying man who is not the wild and powerful and often unpredictable Jesus of Scripture. He was, as Isaiah prophesies, a man of sorrows, yes, but he was also a man of great joy, humor, and formidable authority.[1]

MADELEINE L'ENGLE

I'm so glad I have Cheri in my life, constantly giving me new, living, colorful visions of Christ. I'm also thankful for the Bible, which gives me rainbow-colored pictures of Christ in great detail. Scripture paints a living Lord—with friends, healing, speaking, miracle-making, walking, resting, praying, eating, laughing, telling stories, surprising people with words, wit, and upside-down countercultural ways. When we see Christ through the pages of Scripture we get glimpses of His joyousness, His hilarity, His humanity, and His powerful, divine authority.

One of my favorite stories is found in John 2:1-11. Jesus turns water into wine at a wedding banquet. As I explore the story, I see, hear, taste, touch, and feel what it may have been like to be with Jesus at that banquet in Cana of Galilee. As I'm sure you've surmised by now, my imagination tends to be pretty vivid. First I draw from my personal experience at wedding receptions. I imagine guests in sequined dresses, high-heeled shoes, suits, and hair-sprayed dos. I see dancing, talking, eating, and a fray of frivolity. I also see large mirrors plastered on ballroom walls reflecting the jovial scene. I hear tasteless though danceable music—like the Chicken Dance—blaring from the band. And I smell a strange mélange of cheap perfume, cheap wine, and Chicken Kiev.

My personal wedding reception experiences are superimposed over Jesus' wedding party, bringing a depth and realness to the scene in my mind. As I continue reading, I notice that Christ is in His hometown and that His mother is present. It endears me to Jesus as I picture Him surrounded by family and friends with whom He grew up. There's the aunt who tweaks His cheeks, the grandpa with bad jokes and bad breath, the uncle who always drinks too much, and the second cousin who makes Jesus smile.

The party is cranking along. Bride and groom are dancing, mothers of the bride and groom are gabbing, father of the bride freaking out over how much the shindig is costing. Jesus is swapping stories with His second cousin in a quiet corner when His mom approaches. He can tell by His mama's stride and countenance that something is *terribly* wrong.

Pulling Jesus aside, she yells above the band into His ear,

"They have no more wine!" Backing away from Jesus, she looks imploringly into His eyes, without words saying, "Pleeeeassse do something about this embarrassing situation...I know you can!" Then she disappears into the crowd.

Hesitantly, not wanting to call attention to Himself as the Messiah, Jesus tells the servants to fill six enormous stone jars to the brim with water. Then He tells one of them, "Draw some out and take it to the master of the banquet."

I can just imagine Jesus watching the puzzled and nervous servant walking to the head table with a wine glass filled with water. The master takes the glass, smells the bouquet, gently swirls the liquid around in the glass, and examines the sides for legs. Carefully he takes in a tiny teaser of a taste, swishing it back and forth over thousands of taste buds. The servant stands shaking in his shoes, brow sweaty from worry.

The master raises one eyebrow and takes a hearty gulp of the liquid. He declares to the bride's father loudly enough for the entire hall to hear, "Everyone brings out the choice wine first and then the cheaper wine after the guests have had too much to drink. But you have saved the best till now."

I imagine Christ listening from His favorite corner. He laughs to Himself, humored at being able to do this—His first miracle— to salvage His friend's reception. I also imagine Christ's deeper joy at knowing that His act of kindness is a metaphor of Himself: the Wine of Forgiveness, the Wine that Brings Hope to the Banquet, the Wine to Be Poured Out for Everyone.

I smile, feeling closer to Christ—loving Him more, knowing Him better with each word. I wish I could've been there at that wedding in Cana, and I look forward to the wedding feast where the Wine that Brings Hope will sit at the head table as the Master of the heavenly banquet. Cheri will be there too. We'll toast our own wedding banquets and all the others we've attended in earthly life. And I'm sure when I look into her eyes, the irises will be eclipsed by pupils fully dilated, taking in God face-to-face.

> *Now we see but a poor reflection as in a mirror;*
> *then we shall see face to face.*
>
> 1 CORINTHIANS 13:12

Our Word—*Scriptures, Insights, & Suggestions*

1. What is your image of Jesus? How do your friends and family impact that image? Write about it.

2. How has reading the Bible informed your image of Christ? Are there particular passages in the Gospels that have put flesh and bones on His image for you? Reread those passages when you have a moment. Paraphrase them or journal about them.

3. When you open to the Gospels, do you have a preconceived notion of the Jesus you'll encounter there? If so, write a character description of your preconceived Christ (perhaps in a list form, i.e., gentle, soft-spoken, holy, boring). Then, as you read over the next few months, note any verses or passages that challenge or affirm your view.

> *It is Christ Himself, not the Bible, who is the true word of God. The Bible, read in the right spirit and with the guidance of good teachers, will bring us to Him.*[2]
>
> C.S. LEWIS

Rock Writing

The Bible Gives Good, Solid Words

An anxious heart weighs a [woman] down,
but a kind word cheers [her] up.

PROVERBS 12:25

Her Word—*Stones from Cheri, Margie, and Julie*

A few summers back three of my closest friends—Margie,
Cheri, and Julie—and I got together for a "Hen Party" weekend of
gabbing, eating, praying, walking, and resting. Margie's husband
graciously moved in with a friend for the weekend so we could take
over their home.

On day one, each of the girls and I claimed a room, plopped
down our duffels, and then gathered in the kitchen for sloppy joes,
Waldorf salad, chips, and lemonade. It was so good to eat together
and catch up on life stories. We laughed, lingered, enjoyed each
other.

After lunch Cheri went for a run, Margie took a nap, and Julie
and I continued a ping-pong style tête-à-tête in the family room.

That night we went to a favorite restaurant on the Fox River for
dinner. I wanted to truly savor this rare moment of group cama-
raderie. But starting with the car ride and continuing through the
evening, I was riddled with familiar, searing, burning back pain.

Mid-lumbar, it opened like a rose: crimson, layered, complex. I tried to ignore it as we ate alfresco, watching geese and ducks scoot effortlessly across the river. The pain wouldn't relent. All night I see-sawed between the pleasure of the moment and my physical agony. Several times I wanted to cry. I choked down my tears, not wanting to destroy this special time with my friends.

As we ate and joked and smiled I thought about how I must appear to passersby. No one would imagine the suffering pounding inside me. In the same way, I was probably oblivious to hidden emotional, physical, and relational pain of the strangers sitting beside us on the patio under tranquil, umbrellaed tables.

The next morning my friends and I shared a pot of Margie's French-pressed Brazilian coffee and conversation. That led to a spontaneous hymn and worship song sing around the shiny black baby grand. My girlfriends belted harmonies with great brio that soon inspired a time of prayer.

After the sing, though it felt a little strange, elementary-school-teacheresque, even crazy, I suggested we write one word prayers for each other on rocks I'd gathered during a recent walk. Cheri assuaged my fears when she said she liked the idea. Then Cher added her own creative spin to our time of prayer.

"What do you guys think about doing a 'Rain of Grace' and ending it with Sal's rock prayers?"

"What's a 'Rain of Grace'?" Julie and Margie asked in stereo.

Cheri adeptly explained that it was an exercise she used to do with her theatre group in college. First a woman shares three words that describe struggles or pain she's experiencing. She closes her eyes, and while assuming a stilled position, her friends gather around and repeatedly whisper—even banter—the words as they poke, prod, and pinch her. (I know this sounds a little weird, but the exercise provides a physical exhibition of the ways words affect us.) Next the friends speak *new* words of help, and hope, and healing. As they speak, they feather their fingers down their friend's arms, legs, back, head, and neck.

My jagged black words were *wounded, pained, bound.* As my trio of friends gathered 'round chanting the oppressive words, I began to cry and crumpled into a ball on the ground. They gave me time and space to cry while they wrote words of blessing on the rocks. Then, sensitively, they encircled me again, whispering *"Freedom, peace, breathed...freedom, peace, breathed...freedom, peace, breathed."* Their words echoed and reverberated in my ears as their fingers trickled a "rain of grace" all over me. It felt refreshing, renewing, and light.

Julie handed me the rock inscribed PEACE. Margie, FREEDOM. Cheri, BREATHED.

Each woman received "a rain" and three rocks that morning. I don't think any of us were expecting the reservoir of tears and sharing and grace we experienced. But as the day went on, it was obvious God was with us in a special way in Margie's home, seeing our friendships, our faith, and our personal pains. He vibrated in the timbre of our voices and showed up in our words, written on rocks, for one another.

My rocks now adorn my desk as reminders of the weekend and the prayers of my friends.

> *In Christ we speak before God with sincerity,*
> *like [women] sent from God.*
>
> 2 CORINTHIANS 2:17

God's Word—*Stones of Hope*

> *Every word of God is flawless;*
> *he is a shield to those who take refuge in him.*
>
> PROVERBS 3:5

I have put my hope in your word.

PSALM 119:74

Our friends can be so much like the Bible: active, wordy, creative, life-espousing! Their words have a way of blessing, healing, giving hope, and invigorating us. Because they love us and want what's best for us, they reverberate with the words of blessing God has written on the rock that is His Word.

Each time we crack open the Bible God gives us a promise or plan, a hope or help for our lives. We can hold on to these words as engraved in stone, written by Someone who cares for us. Let's take a quick look at the words given to me by Cheri, Julie, and Margie. As we do, consider these words as God's gifts for all of us.

Freedom

The Greek word for freedom is *eleutheria,* meaning *liberty.* It has a "momentary and comprehensive character."[1] And in Galatians 5:13, which says, "You, my [sisters], were called to be free," it refers to manumission from slavery.

I'm thankful that Margie wished freedom for me. I needed to be reminded that though my physical pain persists, I need not dwell *in* or *on* it. It's not the fullness of who I am. Instead, I'm liberated, released from the domination of pain. It may be part of my life, but it's not stronger than God. And it's not my ultimate end. I can find rest in the knowledge of the freedom that will come in a restored, posthumous body.

Clearly there are days when pain is so overwhelming that Advil, a hot bath, a heating pad, and rest are my only options. But on most days I can choose to be free, focusing on what I have freedom to do—take a restorative walk, read a book to my child, call a friend for more prayer, slowly and carefully cook a meal, set a table, arrange some flowers.

In 2 Corinthians 3:17, Paul uses *eleutheria* when he writes, "Now the Lord is the Spirit, and where the Spirit of the Lord is, there is freedom." Here *eleutheria* "denotes freedom of access to the presence of God."[2] Isn't it comforting to know we have freedom to be near God—our Home, our Help, our ultimate Hope?

We all have places in our lives where we long for more latitude: freedom of health, freedom in spirit, relational freedom, vocational freedom, financial freedom. Let us rest in daily measures of liberty that allow us to draw close to God.

Peace

I'm overwhelmed as I study the connotations of Julie's "peace" offering. When the Greek *eirēnē* occurs in Jesus' words, "Peace I leave with you; my peace I give you" (John 14:27), it means "the sense of rest and contentment."[3] *Wow!* Sometimes, even though I wish my physical ailment would magically disappear, I realize that it slows me down, calling me from a frenetic pace into rest. It's counterintuitive to imagine peace coming from something as annoying and inconvenient as chronic back pain, but God's peace comes in the midst of any circumstance.

How apropos, then, that the title "The God of Peace" is used over and over in the New Testament (i.e., Romans 15:33; Philippians 4:9; 1 Thessalonians 5:23; Hebrews 13:20; 2 Corinthians 13:11).[4] *Vine's* dictionary also notes that the corresponding Hebrew word "*shalom* primarily signifies wholeness," being "unhewn... full...finished...made perfect."[5]

If we look up *hewn* in our good ole Webster's, we find it means "cut with blows of a heavy cutting instrument." So unhewn (and thus "peace") means untouched by a violent, destructive blow. Given this fresh understanding of peace, I wish all of my family, friends, and the women whose paths I cross "*Shalom!* Peace to you!"

Breathed

Some of my favorite stories in the New Testament occur after Jesus dies. In His resurrected realness, Christ makes beachside picnics, takes walks, asks questions, gives promises. According to John, in one of Jesus' first unexpected appearances, He "came and stood among [the disciples] and said, 'Peace be with you!'…And with that he *breathed* on them and said, 'Receive the Holy Spirit'" (John 20:19,22).

When Cheri handed me the word *breathed* written in her tidy, familiar print, I wondered if she had this story in mind. Was she thinking about the Greek word *emphusaō*, which means "to breathe upon"?[6] And the "symbolic act of the Lord Jesus in breathing upon His Apostles the communication of the Holy Spirit"?[7]

As someone who avidly studies and writes about the Bible, I'm sure Cheri knew these facts. But I have a hunch she was really wishing me air and wind and life during a stagnant, stilted season. I'll bet she wanted me to inhale and exhale with the fervor and passion of a woman at peace, a woman set free.

Our Word—*Scriptures, Insights, & Suggestions*

1. If you shared a "Rain of Grace" with your friends, what words do you think they would use to bless you? Write these in your journal.

2. Use a concordance to do a word study on the words you just wrote in your journal. Write down anything that strikes you as true or good or inspiring.

3. If symbols are helpful to you, write these words of encouragement on some stones. Carry them around in your pocket or purse as daily reminders of God's grace that reigns in your life.

4. If you're feeling a little crazy and adventurous, gather some girlfriends for a Hen Party weekend. If the Spirit leads, pray for each other using the "Rain of Grace."

Remember your word to your servant,
for you have given me hope.

PSALM 119:49

Open Arms

Embracing and Embraced by the Word

How long, O LORD, must I call for help, but you do not listen?
Or cry out to you, "Violence!" But you do not save?...
Destruction and violence are before me.

HABAKKUK 1:2-3

Her Word—*Mom Holding the Bible Close*

I grew up in a sunny yellow house with black shutters in one of Chicago's north shore suburbs. From a distance our family life looked idyllic. And in many ways it was. We enjoyed annual vacations, designer clothes, a top-notch education, lavish holidays. To outsiders we looked footloose and free. From an insider's perspective, though, we were a foursome struggling to weed out the wicked generational roots of alcoholism, misogyny, abuse, and rage.

I readily recall living under unreasonable—dare I say draconian—rules and the ever-present fear of wrath that breaking the rules would incur. I also remember frequent shouting and the general stench of air filled with prickly, pervasive tension.

In addition to those not-so-nice memories, I have gentle recollections that sit in my mind like birds nesting on branches of grace. One of these memories is of my mom sitting in a blue family room chair with her Bible draped over her lap like a blanket. At the end of many nights, once the dinner dishes were done and the dishwasher chugged and purred, she'd sit and read. For years Mom studiously and copiously worked her way through hundreds of inductive studies for every book of the Bible. The studies were from Bible Study Fellowship.

I can still hear the sound of Mom turning see-through thin pages as she savored the words as if they were fine chocolates. I have a strong feeling that as Mom read, she brought her questions about the pain in our family before God. I'm sure she asked Him to make sense out of the cyclical sins of abuse and codependency in our family.

One year, as the family prepared for our annual fishing trip to Arkansas, Mom had her heart set on studying Habakkuk (an Old Testament prophet). As she packed her Bible, she asked if I wanted to join her in the study. "We could do it early in the morning when Dad and Rob will be out on the lake fishing," she encouraged.

Never having read Habakkuk, I jammed my huge, brown Ryrie Study Bible into my bag and we were off. With enthusiasm and expectancy, I welcomed the invitation.

Through our sunrise study, Mom and I gleaned much truth about Judah and Babylon, the kings Jehoiakim and Nebuchadnezzar. But when I think back on our learning, what I remember most fondly is what we discovered about Habakkuk's name. It means "embracer." It is said that Habakkuk was given this name because he embraced God's people and God's providence even in the face of the evil in the world. During difficult times Habakkuk, like my mom, asked God tough questions...and then he embraced God's good and faithful love and provision.

> *Lord, I have heard the report about You and I fear.*
> *O Lord, revive Your work in the midst of the years...*
> *make it known; in wrath remember mercy.*
>
> Habakkuk 3:2 nasb

God's Word—*Squeezing Back*

> *There is strife, and conflict abounds. Therefore the law is paralyzed, and justice never prevails. The wicked hem in the righteous, so that justice is perverted.*
>
> HABAKKUK 1:3-4

Habakkuk, the embracer, found himself living during evil days. The Babylonians, a ruthless savage nation, were overtaking Judah. It was a time of international crisis and corruption. Though I hardly think living in an abusive home can be perfectly paralleled with the injustice, violence, and evil surrounding Habbakuk during the destruction under the Babylonians, I do think there are some valuable comparisons.

Anyone who is oppressed wonders why God, a redemptive Savior, allows the oppression to continue. Anyone who is the victim of anger, abuse, or rage cries out to God for help and answers. Anyone who lives in fear longs for freedom. This is why Habakkuk boldly questions God about the fate of Judah, "You cannot tolerate wrong. Why then do you tolerate the treacherous? Why are you silent while the wicked swallow up those more righteous than themselves?" (Habakkuk 1:13). For two chapters God and "the embracer" parlay and debate. Then God gives an answer. It's not the answer for which Habakkuk, or my mom, originally hoped. It doesn't come in a treatise, thesis, or even a simple sentence. But, as Ronald Blue notes in the *Bible Knowledge Commentary,* Habakkuk's "ever-present 'Why?'" is ultimately "answered by the everlasting 'Who?'"[1]

By the end of his book and having talked feverishly with God, laying all his questions on the line, Habakkuk embraces God's every word. Habakkuk knows God is ultimately in control. He knows that even when evil looks victorious, God is the ultimate champion. Habakkuk wraps his mind and warm arms around these realities. He's the embracer.

This reminds me of the way my mom, in the midst of a difficult season, sat with God and His Word in her blue chair. Both Habakkuk and Mom questioned God in the face of injustice. He heard them. In the end, they both chose to take God at His word. They open their arms wide, hugging the Truth through thick and thin. They embrace the fact that though God allows Babylonian sieges and family strife, He is still sovereign. They believe He will ultimately "intervene with great force, shaking the very foundations of the earth until no sign of injustice remains."[2] As we open God's Word, looking for answers to life's difficult questions, may we also open our arms and be known as "embracers."

I just returned from sharing Thanksgiving weekend with Bryan, my children, my brother, his wife, and my folks. During years of precarious and estranged relationships, I never imagined this day would come. It is a wonder that the nine of us were all in the same house at the same time. It was a miracle that we actually enjoyed each other—breaking bread, telling jokes, being kind in peace and honor and emotional well being. Though we all still have quirks, differences, childhood scars, and a bit of crazy stubbornness at times, God honored His words. He "came out to deliver [His] people" (Habakkuk 3:13). And as we've taken my mom's lead in embracing God, He has brought us closer in His almighty embrace.

Our Word—*Scriptures, Insights, & Suggestions*

> *Continue seeking Him with seriousness. Unless he wanted you, you would not be wanting him.*[3]
>
> C.S. Lewis

1. Select a life verse, a month verse, or a day verse. Write it on a 3 x 5 card or in a journal. Study it, meditate on it, memorize it. Let the words and truth help you experience God's embrace.

2. When you read the Bible, make your time special by lighting a candle, sitting in a special chair, draping yourself with a cozy blanket. Sip your favorite juice or enjoy fresh fruit as you read. Feel the warm embrace of every sacred second!

> *I turn to the Bible in fear and trembling,*
> *trying to see it whole, not using it for my own purposes,*
> *but letting its ongoing message of love direct me.*[4]
>
> MADELEINE L'ENGLE

Shared Stories

God's Word Connects Us

Stories, no matter how simple, can be vehicles of truth...
It's no coincidence that Jesus taught almost entirely by
telling stories, simple stories dealing with the stuff of
life...to help us become more whole.[1]

MADELEINE L'ENGLE

Her Word—*Margie's Peonies and the Black Ants*

Last summer Margie and her two children stopped by for crepes. The peonies were blooming beside our deck, so I cut a few, stuck them in a Mason jar with cold water, and placed them on the table beside a stack of Fiestaware plates. Within seconds an army of big black ants leaped out of the pale pink blossoms like paratroopers, adding unsolicited decorations to my spread. Frantically I swatted the black buggers with napkins. Oblivious to their impending deaths, they seemed to dance in time to Susan Ashton's voice crooning a country-remix from my family room.

As I killed what I hoped was the last six-legged creeper with the heel of my sandal, I remembered that the ants had infested my peonies last spring...and the spring before. I wondered why the critters were attracted to these particular flowers and wished I'd left the bouquet—along with its inhabitants—on the bush outside.

When Margie and her brood arrived, one of the first things she said was, "Wow, Sal, those peonies are *beautiful*..." Then she bent over to sniff the largest bloom. "And so aromatic." As she sniffed I feared one last stowaway would leap onto the bridge of her nose.

"They *are* pretty," I said. "But they were also home to about a dozen enormous black ants, which I killed right before you pulled up."

The green in Margie's eyes intensified with a memory. She adjusted the baby on her lap. I could tell she was about to share one of her multitudes of stories.

"As a child I used to love cutting Mom's peonies," she began wistfully. "I'd bring them into the house by the basketful. My favorite thing was to arrange them in a vase in the kitchen and then wait for ants to emerge. After peaking out, the ants would jump to the white table, scurrying about, looking like a living dot-to-dot. I remember trying to connect the critters with imaginary lines, but they moved too fast."

Until that very moment I thought I was the only one whose peonies attracted ants. *Everyone's peonies probably attract big, black ants!* I thought. *What an epiphany!* That may not sound like an enormous insight, but in the moment it seemed like a flash of enlightenment. Realizing that I wasn't the only one on the planet who simultaneously dealt with beauty and the real stuff of life—mosquito bites, inconvenience, iniquity, pain, and black ants—was extremely comforting.

As Margie sat in the family room with the kids, I filled crepes with strawberries and thought of some of the other stories Margie and I have shared. We've walked with each other through college and cancer, breakups and weddings, funerals and births. She was there after my father-in-law took his last breath. I was there when her son took his first. Together we've dealt with financial struggles, unexpected gifts, broken dreams, extended family freak-outs, forgiveness and healing, jealousy and joy. All pictures of pain framed in beauty.

Jesus told His friends, "In this world you will have trouble. But take heart!" (John 16:33). Peter, Andrew, James, John, Mary Magdalene...and Margie and I have found this to be true. Knowing we're not alone in the world and telling one another of our pains—sharing our stories—helps us heal and take heart.

I'm glad Margie told me about her ants. I'm glad she let me into her life as her husband wrestled with brain cancer. I'm also glad she walked with me though a huge rift in my family. I so appreciate her support in the years of excruciating back pain. I wish neither Margie nor I had black ants in our peonies. But since trouble, pain, and difficulty often accompany beauty, I'm thankful to have a friend for the journey—a friend who is honest, wise, and free-wheeling with her stories.

> *Let's recover our story because we'll die without it.*
> *It's a life-giving story—this magnificent narrative we*
> *find in Scripture—if we are willing to read openly*
> *and to read all of Scripture, not just passages selected to*
> *help us prove our point...God did indeed send his*
> *only begotten son to come live with us, as one of us,*
> *to help us understand our stories—each one unique,*
> *infinitely valuable, irreplaceable.*[2]
>
> MADELEINE L'ENGLE

God's Word—*The Greatest Story Ever Told*

> *I am who I am because my friendships keep on*
> *growing—because there are always new people slipping*
> *into my life, new voices, new stories...*[3]
>
> BETH KEPHART

> *My story and your story are all part of each other...*
> *if only because we have sung together and prayed together*
> *and seen each other's faces...in other words all our stories*
> *are in the end one story, one vast story about being*
> *human, being together, being here.*[4]
>
> FREDERICK BUECHNER

In the same way Margie is full of stories that help me deal with life's pain, so is the Bible. It's packed with tales of murder, incest, adultery, love triangles, abandonment, adoption, love, lies, good conquering evil. Anytime we feel alone in our personal pain, we can turn to the Bible and find someone who has gone through troubles similar to ours. What a gift to have a book filled with stories of men and women who've walked with God...and each other... through life's trials.

Here are a couple of my favorite stories about biblical women. Their snapshots have been pasted into the scrapbook of my life much like Margie's have.

Moses' Mom

For nine months Moses' mom carried her beloved baby boy. During his gestation she suffered inchworm-like stretch marks on her belly, tsunami-sized waves of nausea, and ultimately a labor sans epidural. After three months of hiding her ravenous child in the warmth of a nursing nook, she's forced to bring her infant boy to the chilly banks of the Nile where she must yank him off her breast and float him down the green river in an unreliable, papyrus basket-boat (Exodus 2). It smells of fresh tar and pitch. She worries about the fumes but knows this fate is not as bad as death under Pharaoh's hands.

Weeping tears of saline and milk, she watches her baby's precarious float. Drifting away from the bank, Moses shines a first social smile at his mom. It lifts her to the sun. She crashes when the smile quickly turns to wailing as the babe loses sight of his mama. Her relief lights afresh when Moses' sister brings word that Pharaoh's beautiful daughter has discovered baby Moses in his badly water-logged bassinet. And rejoicing brims like a fountain when further word comes that the princess desires a nursemaid—and Moses' biological mother gets the job!

Little do either of the mothers know that through the twists and turns of adoptive grace, each will journey deeper into the rewards of letting go, the surprising joys of motherhood, and the deep wonders of a life of faith. Led by their wise, God-centered son, they'll discover holiness in a very human way. Just as the princess drew Moses out of the water, so will their child draw faith-filled depths out of them.

As a newly adoptive mother of one of China's lost daughters, I feel connected to Pharaoh's daughter and have compassion for Moses' biological mama. These women probably wouldn't have chosen an adoptive path for their lives. Neither would I. But the three of us have been enlarged by the unexpected joys and connections forged by our adoptive journeys. The story of my life is enriched by reading theirs. Connected through centuries and cultures, we all have one thing in common: Our hearts have been expanded by pain and beauty.

Mary Magdalene

One of Jesus' dearest friends, Mary Magdalene—the first person to see Christ after He rose from the dead—was a weeper. Instead of going back to her home like the twelve disciples did after Jesus was placed in the tomb, Mary "stood outside the tomb crying. As she wept, she bent over to look into the tomb" (John 20:11).

I imagine her cries being loud and long, unabashedly mournful, strong, empty, resolute. Thinking Jesus gone for good, Mary sat weeping. With each shudder, gasp, and sigh, I'll bet she relived the things Christ taught her: that the kingdom of heaven is at hand, that the last shall be first, that mustard-seed faith matters, that those who mourn are blessed.

Her cries echoed off the tomb's stone walls until Jesus appeared and asked, "Woman, why are you crying?" (John 20:13). After a head-bowed, tear-drenched explanation, Mary looked at Jesus. He called her by name and she shrieked, "Rabboni!" Teacher. That's the name weeping Mary Magdalene called her dear friend at this life-after-death moment. *Teacher.*

He was her teacher just as He is mine. When I think of Christ as my Teacher my heart flutters. Having worked in academia for more than a decade, it's easy and natural for me to connect with Christ like Mary did...as a student. Both of us, along with millions of others across this blue-and-green globe, feel this way. We love learning. We search and find direction, hope, and meaning in Christ's life and words. As His students we're connected because we've opened our ears, hearts, and lives to Him.

Like Mary, we remember Jesus' stories and enjoy a special teacher–student intimacy that causes us to weep at the thought of His crucifixion. Like pumps primed by loving leadership, creative examples, dynamic didactics, our eyes have been opened to see truth and let tears flow.

Not everyone connects with the story of Mary Magdalene, Moses' mama, or Margie's peonies the way I do. But the pages of Scripture hold story after story as plentiful and powerful as rolling ocean waves. They connect us to God, to biblical characters, and to each other. Reading through the Bible in search of a tale that's personally pertinent at that moment in time is like hunting for a treasure trove.

Whether the story of Cain and Abel helps heal sibling rivalry... Jacob, Rachel, and Leah's love triangle sheds light on an entangled relationship...Hannah's struggle with becoming a mother gives encouragement during an infertile season...or Paul's suffering scale-eradicating sojourn brings hope for new visions, when we read God's Word looking for connections, searching for the ways our stories parallel those of biblical heroes and heroines, we discover we're not alone. We live in a community of shared experience. And the people who have gone before us travel with us through life like wise, faithful friends.

> *The Bible is a book about you and me, who God made and lost and continually seeks, so you might say that what holds it together more than anything else is us. You might add to that, of course, that of all the books that humanity has produced, it is the one which...also holds us together.*[5]
>
> FREDERICK BUECHNER

Our Word—*Scriptures, Insights, & Suggestions*

> *How many years did I live beside my neighbor before I could engage myself in the jumble of her hippie days, her wedding on a Korean hill, the fables of the mill town where she grew up?*[6]
>
> BETH KEPHART

1. Is there a Bible story you feel particularly connected with? What is the story? Why does it speak to you? Write about this.

2. When you have time, read through Moses' abandonment story (Exodus 2:1-10) or the story of Mary Magdalene and the Risen Christ (John 20:10-18). Is there anything in the lives of these women that parallels yours? Explain.

3. Reread some of your favorite Bible stories. As you read, be open to fresh insights. Sketch or paint a scene from a story and look for details you may have overlooked. Or paraphrase a story to

bring the text to life. Be free with this. Try new directions. Enjoy the process and see what you discover!

4. Have a friend over for coffee. Share some of your stories. Discuss ways your stories intersect or parallel the stories of biblical heroes and the help that brings to you.

> *In the long run the stories all overlap and mingle like searchlights in the dark. The stories Jesus tells are part of the story Jesus is, and the other way around.*
> *And the story Jesus is, is part of the story you and I are because Jesus has become so much a part of the world's story that it is impossible to imagine how any of our stories would have turned out without him.*[7]
>
> FREDERICK BUECHNER

Epilogue

I do my writing in a closet—yes, literally a closet. On the wall I've stapled hundreds of my favorite pictures. Emily and I with teary eyes, both dressed serendipitously in jade green, standing in a Chinese Civil Affairs office on the day we officially became mother and daughter. A close-up of Heather in her crazed normalcy, rubbing a pearl from the strand I brought her from China on an exposed front tooth. Cheri and I at Margie's baby shower, placing hands of blessing on a nine-month-pregnant beach ball belly. My editor, Barb Gordon, smiling as she floats in azure waters beside a similarly smiling dolphin. My cousin Elaina making a wish on a dandelion gone to seed. Each picture telling a story. Each story becoming part of my story.

Sometimes when I'm taking a mental break from writing, I look at my picture wall. Lately, as I've been writing this book, when I explore the pictures I wonder what my wall would be like if it were covered with the faces of Adam and Eve, Jesus and His 12 buds, Mary and Martha, Abraham and Sara, Hagar, Cain and Abel—all the people I've met through the pages of God's Book. Then I lean back and realize that in a way my wall *is* covered with these folks.

Behind the crying eyes of Emily and me is the picture of Moses and Pharaoh's daughter, and even of baby Jesus, who was adopted by Joseph. Behind the expectant smile of pregnant Margie are thousands of expectant women, including Mary, Sarah, Elizabeth,

Hagar, and Hannah. Hidden behind Elaina's childlike-dandelion-wish are the wishes and dreams of Joseph, David, and Jairus' daughter. Through shared experience and journeys with God, all our stories have been pasted into a cosmic scrapbook that reaches beyond space and time.

Just yesterday this idea that our stories are connected with each other's and with biblical people was reinforced. I returned from my mailbox with an undesirable load of catalogs (which I recycled) and my ever-precious first Christmas card of the year. In order to savor the card, I prepared some cocoa and sat down in the overstuffed chair in my front room. On the card's cover was a bucolic rendition of the Nativity. Mary, cloaked in pale indigo, bent cautiously and maternally over baby Jesus. Joseph seeming to pace nervously in the background.

I opened the card to find the inscription in cheery red: *For unto us a child is born. Unto us a Son is given.* Immediately Handel's setting of this text, The Messiah, leaped into my head. The melody bounced around my brain like a rubber ball. While enjoying my mental orchestra, I read the Christmas letter enclosed in the card. The opening line: *It has been an exciting year for us as we're expecting a baby boy in the spring!*

I almost laughed out loud thinking about my expectant friend choosing *this* card during *this* precisely pregnant moment. An epiphany fell on me like snow. My girlfriend was sending me, and all those on her Christmas card list, the story of her own nativity right along with the seasonal declaration of Christ's Nativity.

I don't know, dear reader, what God is birthing in your personal nativity. But my prayer for you is that as you close this book you'll see yourself in Christ's story. I hope you find yourself sharing your stories…and God's stories…with family and friends. As you do, may you experience fully the Word that lightens your path, feeds and sustains, salves, writes on your heart, inspires, tells the truth, comforts, heals, and holds promises for your life.

Notes

Chapter 1—Getting to Know You

1. Madeleine L'Engle and Luci Shaw, *Friends for the Journey* (Ann Arbor, MI: Servant Publications, 1997), p. 32.

2. Lauren F. Winner, *Girl Meets God* (Chapel Hill, NC: Algonquin Books of Chapel Hill, 2002), p. 256.

3. Richard J. Foster, *Celebration of Discipline: The Path to Spiritual Growth* (San Francisco: Harper & Row Publishers, 1978), pp. 61-62.

Chapter 2—Word Balloons

1. Frederick Buechner, *A Room Called Remember: Uncollected Pieces* (San Francisco: Harper & Row Publishers, 1984), p. 180.

2. Ibid., pp. 180-81.

3. A.W. Tozer. *The Pursuit of God* (Camp Hill: Christian Publications, Inc., 1982), p. 73.

Chapter 3—Touch, Smell, Taste, Read, and See

1. Madeleine L'Engle, *Penguins & Golden Calves: Icons and Idols in Antarctica and Other Unexpected Places* (Colorado Springs: WaterBrook Press, 2003), pp. 79, 81-82.

2. Ibid., p. 8.

3. Brennan Manning, *The Ragamuffin Gospel* (Sisters, OR: Multnomah Publishers, 2000), p. 95.

4. L'Engle, *Penguins,* p. 233.

5. Ibid., p. 236.

6. Madeleine L'Engle and Luci Shaw, *Friends for the Journey* (Ann Arbor, MI: Servant Publications, 1997), pp. 49-50.

Chapter 4—Heart Scribbles

1. Sally Miller and Cheri Mueller, *Walk with Me: Two Friends on a Spiritual Journey* (Grand Haven, MI: FaithWalk Publishing, 2005), p. 79.

2. Madeleine L'Engle and Luci Shaw, *Friends for the Journey* (Ann Arbor, MI: Servant Publications, 1997), p. 51.

3. Trent Butler, gen. ed., *Holman Bible Dictionary* (Nashville: Holman Bible Publishers, 1991), p. 873.

Chapter 5—You Can Call Me...

1. Madeleine L'Engle, *The Rock That Is Higher: Story as Truth* (Colorado Springs: Shaw Books, 2002), p. 236.

2. Ibid.

3. Joyce Sackett, *In God's Garden* (Wheaton, IL: Tyndale House Publishers, 1998), p. 32.

4. Ibid.

Chapter 6—A Theme Runs Through It

1. Patrick Gardner, *SPARKNOTES for John Milton's Paradise Lost* (New York: SparkNotes, 2002), p. 19.

2. Laurence Perrine, *Story and Structure* (New York: Harcourt Brace, 1983), p. 106.

3. Frederick Buechner, *A Room Called Remember: Uncollected Pieces* (San Francisco: Harper & Row, 1984), pp. 180-81.

4. W.E. Vine, *Vine's Expository Dictionary of New Testament Words* (Peabody, MA: Hendrickson Publishers, n.d.), p. 703.

5. C.S. Lewis, *A Grief Observed* (New York: Bantam Books, 1976), p. 31.

6. Anne Lamott, *Traveling Mercies* (New York: Anchor Books, 2000), p. 241.

7. Madeleine L'Engle, *The Rock That Is Higher: Story as Truth* (Colorado Springs: Shaw Books, 2002), p. 122.

Chapter 7—Great Physicians

1. Henri J.M. Nouwen, *Compassion: A Reflection on the Christian Life* (New York: Image Books, 1983), p. 13.

2. Ibid., p. 27.

3. Madeleine L'Engle and Luci Shaw, *Friends for the Journey* (Ann Arbor, MI: Servant Publications, 1997), p. 48.

4. Nouwen, *Compassion,* p. 27.

5. Madeleine L'Engle, *Two-Part Invention* (San Francisco: Harper Collins, 1989), pp. 123-24.

Chapter 8—Frequent Flyers

1. C.S. Lewis, *Studies in Medieval and Renaissance Literature,* ed. by Walter Hooper (Cambridge: Cambridge University Press, 1967), p. 2.

2. Ibid., pp. 2-3.

3. Ann M. Martin, *A Corner of the Universe* (New York: Scholastic Press, 2002), p. 189.

Chapter 9—Family Ties

1. Grace Lin, *The Year of the Dog* (New York: Little, Brown and Company, 2006), pp. 135-36.

2. Lauren F. Winner, *Girl Meets God* (Chapel Hill, NC: Algonquin Books of Chapel Hill, 2002), p. 270.

Chapter 10—Red Reminders

1. Sue Monk Kidd, *When the Heart Waits* (New York: HarperCollins, 1990), p. 15.

Chapter 11—Loving Your Neighbor

1. Henry Nouwen, *Compassion* (New York: Image Books, 1983).

Chapter 12—A True Page-Turner

1. Liz Curtis Higgs, *Slightly Bad Girls of the Bible* (Colorado Springs: WaterBrook Press, 2007).
2. Madeleine L'Engle, *The Rock That Is Higher: Story as Truth* (Colorado Springs: Shaw Books, 2002), pp. 293-94.
3. Ibid., p. 122.

Chapter 13—I Give You My Word

1. Michael Card, *Immanuel: Reflections on the Life of Christ* (Nashville: Thomas Nelson Publishers, 1981), p. 24.
2. Ibid.
3. Ibid.

Chapter 14—Glow Sticks

1. Madeleine L'Engle, *Bright Evening Star: Mystery of the Incarnation* (Colorado Springs: Shaw Books, 1997), pp. 190-91.

Chapter 15—Spices, Perfumes, Stories

1. Ann Spangler and Jean E. Syswerda, *Women of the Bible: A One-Year Devotional Study of Women in Scripture* (Grand Rapids, MI: Zondervan, 1999), p. 13.
2. Ibid., p. 395.

Chapter 16—Filling in the Blanks

1. Beth Kephart, *Into the Tangle of Friendship* (New York: Houghton Mifflin, 2000), p. 178.
2. Ibid., p. 55.
3. Madeleine L'Engle, *The Rock That Is Higher: Story as Truth* (Colorado Springs: Shaw Books, 2002), pp. 217-18.
4. Madeleine L'Engle and Luci Shaw, *Friends for the Journey* (Ann Arbor, MI: Servant Publications, 1997), p. 48.

Chapter 17—Unexpected Friends

1. Sally Miller and Cheri Mueller, *Walk with Me: Two Friends on a Spiritual Journey* (Grand Haven, MI: FaithWalk Publishing, 2005), p. v.
2. Cheri's written version of this story appears on page 170 of *Walk with Me: Two Friends on a Spiritual Journey,* the first book Cher and I coauthored.
3. Sue Monk Kidd, *When the Heart Waits* (New York: HarperCollins, 1990), p. 54.
4. Ibid.

Chapter 18—Expectant Friends

1. Sue Monk Kidd, *When the Heart Waits* (New York: HarperCollins, 1990), pp. 28-29.
2. Ibid., p. 14.
3. Ibid.

Chapter 19—Freedom Within Boundaries

1. Susan Newman, *Little Things Long Remembered: Making Your Children Feel Special Every Day* (New York: Crown Publishers, 1993), p. 11.
2. Trent Butler, gen. ed., *Holman Bible Dictionary* (Nashville: Holman Bible Publishers, 1991), p. 367.
3. Madeleine L'Engle, *The Rock That Is Higher: Story as Truth* (Colorado Springs: Shaw Books, 2002), p. 43.
4. Oswald Chambers, *My Utmost for His Highest* (Grand Rapids, MI: Discovery House Publishers, 1992), August 14.

Chapter 21—Dream Catchers

1. Sue Monk Kidd, *When the Heart Waits* (New York: HarperCollins, 1990), p. 15.
2. Ibid.

Chapter 22—God's Garden

1. Tovah Martin, *Tasha Tudor's Garden* (Boston: Houghton Mifflin, 1994).
2. Joyce Sackett, *In God's Garden* (Wheaton, IL: Tyndale House Publishers, 1998), pp. 121-22.
3. Ibid., p. 122.

Chapter 23—Sustaining Meals

1. Oswald Chambers, *My Utmost for His Highest* (Grand Rapids, MI: Discovery House Publishers, 1992), February 2.
2. Ibid., February 9.
3. Madeleine L'Engle and Luci Shaw, *Friends for the Journey* (Ann Arbor, MI: Servant Publications, 1997), p. 117.

Chapter 25—Eyes

1. Madeleine L'Engle, *The Rock That Is Higher: Story as Truth* (Colorado Springs: Shaw Books, 2002), p. 121.
2. C.S. Lewis, *The Letters of C.S. Lewis* (New York: Harcourt Brace, 1966), p. 247.

Chapter 26—Rock Writing

1. W.E. Vine, *Vine's Expository Dictionary of New Testament Words* (Peabody, MA: Hendrickson Publishers, n.d.), p. 471.

2. Ibid.

3. Ibid., p. 852.

4. Ibid.

5. Ibid.

6. Ibid., p. 151.

7. Ibid.

Chapter 27—Open Arms

1. Quoted in John F. Walvoord and Roy B. Zuck, eds., *The Bible Knowledge Commentary* (Wheaton, IL: Victor Books, 1985), p. 1505.

2. Philip Yancey and Brenda Quinn, *Meet the Bible: A Panorama of God's Word in 366 Daily Readings and Reflections* (Grand Rapids, MI: Zondervan Publishing House, 2001), p. 322.

3. C.S. Lewis, *Letters of C.S. Lewis* (New York: Harcourt/Harvest Books, 2003), p. 233.

4. Madeleine L'Engle, *The Rock That Is Higher: Story as Truth* (Colorado Springs: Shaw Books, 2002), pp. 64-65.

Chapter 28—Shared Stories

1. Madeleine L'Engle, *Walking on Water: Reflections on Faith and Art* (Wheaton, IL: Harold Shaw Publishers, 1980), pp. 45-46.

2. Madeleine L'Engle, *The Rock That Is Higher: Story as Truth* (Colorado Springs: Shaw Books, 2002), pp. 216-17.

3. Beth Kephart, *Into the Tangle of Friendship* (New York: Houghton Mifflin, 2000), pp. 54-55.

4. Frederick Buechner, *The Clown in the Belfry* (San Francisco: HarperCollins, 1992), p. 137.

5. Ibid., p. 44.

6. Kephart, *Tangle,* p. 62.

7. Buechner, *Clown,* p. 137.

Girl Talk...God Talk

Sally Miller

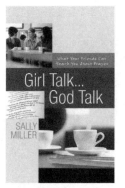

With God as your friend you can...

- share openly
- talk freely
- feel completely at ease
- laugh together
- receive grace and love

Through refreshing stories and sparkling relationships, Sally Miller invites you to consider prayer in the light of friendship—as intimate, fun, serious, and encouraging. As you explore the blessing and strengths of friends, you'll discover how they reflect the love and care of our Lord and Savior.

Girlfriend interactions bring joy to your life,
but even greater happiness awaits when you
experience friendship with God!

Other Great Harvest House Reading

WHEN YOUR PAST IS HURTING YOUR PRESENT
Sue Augustine

Is your past dictating your present and future? Do you want to break this destructive pattern and move on to a happier life? Sue Augustine was once held captive by a painful past. With compassion, empathy, and a touch of humor, she shows you how to identify, release, and change how you respond to the past; overcome a "victim" stance; trade bitterness for peace and joy, set goals with passion and purpose, and understand God's incredible timing and direction. Cut loose the baggage of long-ago...and see your fears conquered, your dreams renewed, your future bright with possibilities.

DESIGNING YOUR HOME ON A BUDGET
Emilie Barnes and Yoli Brogger with Anne Christian Buchanan

Learn the rules and how to break them. Find bargains. Love the results. Revealing the keys to decorating beautifully on a budget, Emilie and Yoli provide basic design principles and ways to implement or break them to create a unique style. You'll discover how to do the things that establish a comfortable, inviting home, such as adding little touches to liven up a room, knowing when to refurbish and when to buy new, finding affordable new and used treasures, and making a child's room fun.

HOW TO TALK TO YOUR KIDS ABOUT DRUGS
Stephen Arterburn and Jim Burns

With straight talk about the situations kids like yours face, bestselling authors Arterburn and Burns present 6 key factors in drug abuse and proven techniques for prevention, the signs of drug use, information for intervention, and how to deal with kids on drugs. *How to Talk to Your Kids About Drugs* provides the knowledge and tools you need to help your kids stay or become drug-free. Includes a helpful study guide for personal use and group discussion.

THE MOM I WANT TO BE
T. Suzanne Eller

Your life is influenced by the mothering you received as a child. If neglect or inconsistency was a part of your upbringing, you need a healthy vision of the wonderful thing motherhood can be. Suzie Eller gently, compassionately gives you a godly, nurturing model. From her own difficult experience, she reveals how bitterness and anger can be transformed into hope. She also shows how shattered legacies can be put back together; explores ways to forgive, let go, and leave your baggage in the past; and offers ways to give your kids the gift of good memories and a great future.

RED-HOT MONOGAMY: MAKING YOUR MARRIAGE SIZZLE
Bill and Pam Farrel

Did you know that the best sexual experiences are enjoyed by married couples? Marriage and relationship experts Bill and Pam reveal what you need to know to add sizzle to your love life. You'll discover...God specifically designed you to give and receive pleasure from your mate, a little skill turns marriage into red-hot monogamy, sex works best when approached emotionally, physically, and physiologically. Along with ways to create intimacy when you're tired and how to avoid "pleasure thieves," you'll find hundreds of ideas to inspire romance and passion in every aspect of your relationship.

MEN ARE LIKE WAFFLES—WOMEN ARE LIKE SPAGHETTI
Bill and Pam Farrel

Bill and Pam explain why a man is like a waffle (each element of his life is in a separate box), why a woman is like spaghetti (everything in her life touches everything else), and what these differences mean. Biblical insights, sound research, humorous anecdotes, and real-life stories make this guide entertaining and practical. Discover how to let gender differences work for you, achieve fulfillment in romantic relationships, and coordinate parenting so kids receive good, consistent care. Much of the material in this rewarding book will also improve interactions with family, friends, and coworkers.

A WOMAN AFTER GOD'S OWN HEART®
Elizabeth George

Become the woman of excellence God designed you to be! Genuine peace and joy come when women follow God in every area of their lives—and become women after His heart. With warmth and grace, Elizabeth George shares practical, scriptural insights on how you can pursue God's priorities concerning your walk with the Lord, your ministry, your home, your husband, and your children. Allow God to transform you by preparing your heart and mind to embrace His incredible work.

HARVEST HOUSE
PUBLISHERS